THE SUNDAY TIMES

Performance Appraisals

Bob Havard

KOGAN PAGE | *CREATING SUCCESS*

To Fran, Ellen, Owen and my mother Tillie Havard

Acknowledgements go to Fran Havard, Julia Steward, Mike Dutfield, Chris Eling, Frank Hayter, Peter Needham, Howard Hudson and Frank Hartle.

First published in 2001

Kogan Page Limited
120 Pentonville Road
London N1 9JN

The views expressed in this book are those of the author, and are not necessarily the same as those of Times Newspapers Ltd.

British Library Cataloguing in Publication Data

A CIP record for this book is available from the British Library.

ISBN 0 7494 3319 1

Cover design by DW Design, London
Typeset by Jean Cussons Typesetting, Diss, Norfolk
Printed and bound in Great Britain by Clays Ltd, St Ives plc

contents

preface

Successful organisations are hungry for feedback. They became successful because of that hunger. Teams and individuals can display the same determination to succeed. Successful teams put considerable energy into assessing their performance and impact. Team leaders and members share information from internal and external customers and from suppliers. They celebrate success and plan for improvement. Successful individuals are often equally voracious in their appetite for feedback. They gather data both formally and informally. They do not rely on an annual appraisal to find out how they are doing. Usually they already know! For them, the organisation's appraisal process is, at best, a useful supplement to the feedback mechanisms they have developed for themselves, and a useful way of taking stock and developing or adjusting plans for their future action. At worst, if the organisation's review process is deficient, it may reduce their commitment to the organisation.

This book is about the performance appraisal approaches and mechanisms that help successful organisations to build on their success and to generate and meet the desire for feedback. The book also acts as a guide for organisations that are currently performing less well and want to do the things that successful organisations do. In addition, it aims to support individual managers who want to use performance appraisal to help them achieve their goals through the people working to them, in the absence of, or in spite of, their organisation's appraisal processes. It will help those who are introducing changes to an appraisal process.

When I refer to 'organisations' I am including businesses, not-for-profit, and government organisations. 'People' within the organisation include staff, employees, associates, volunteers in charities – anyone who contributes to the work of the organisation.

The book pays most attention to ways of designing and using performance appraisal processes for individuals. I will demonstrate that to deliver results for an organisation, appraisal needs to be part of a comprehensive approach to managing organisational performance. Properly designed and implemented, performance appraisal can bring life and vitality to individual performance and create excellence. My intention is to steer readers through the issues. The aim is to provide a 'how to go about it' book to help those charged with introducing or revamping appraisal to decide what needs to be in place for appraisal to deliver benefits to the organisation. It will help to get those things into place, and help plan and action the introduction or reinvigoration of an appraisal process.

Central to this book are the notions that appraisal:

■ draws on, and can bring together, other aspects of performance management – objectives, targets, etc;
■ is used to take stock of an individual's performance;
■ covers a known review period;
■ has at its core a face-to-face appraisal discussion;
■ uses an informed appraiser;
■ usually occurs at least once a year;
■ provides an opportunity to recognise performance;
■ results in an action plan for performance maintenance or improvement, eg through clarifying objectives, coaching, monitoring, training and development goals.

about the author

Bob Havard, MA, MPhil, FCIPD, has run his own management consultancy practice since 1988, working in the public, private and not-for-profit sectors. Havard Consulting helps clients to link the development of individuals, teams and the whole organisation. Earlier in his career, Bob worked in EMI's Personnel Department at the time the Beatles were still recording and was a Training Officer with Philips Electronics in the early 1970s. He has also worked for a youth and social work agency, lectured at two universities and was a management trainer and consultant in a management college. He has had a wide range of clients, including Pearl Assurance, Groupe Schneider, Barnados, the Ministry of Defence and a social services department.

He has helped introduce appraisal and performance management processes into client organisations and has trained well over 1,000 people in appraisal skills.

Other assignments have involved assessing organisational capability, assisting the successful merger of three companies, leadership and management development, HR strategy, profiling people-management practices, innovation management, making top team appointments and applying the EFQM Excellence Model. He is a Fellow and a registered consultant of the Chartered Institute of Personnel and Development, a licensed user of the Emotional Competence Inventory and a member of the British Psychological Society.

Bob can be contacted at:
Havard Consulting
41 St Martins Road
Knowle
Bristol BS4 2NQ

Tel/fax: +44 (0) 117 9770050

excellence and managing performance

what excellent organisations do well

This book aims to support organisations that want to use performance appraisal to help them to be acknowledged as, and remain, excellent organisations. Therefore, it is helpful to identify how excellent organisations operate.

---

the excellent garage

Andy runs a repair and maintenance garage. Over the last 20 years he has moved from employing one other person to employing 8, and now has custom-built premises. The garage has always specialised in Citroëns and Peugeots and has a very loyal customer base. Andy is straight dealing and always looking to offer a practical, quality service at the lowest cost locally, without taking risky shortcuts.

He spends time talking to customers and listening attentively to their needs.

Recently he decided to sell tyres. He recognises that although he cannot match the prices of specialist tyre-fitting firms and makes little money from tyre sales, it is more convenient for his customers if he has a stock of the standard tyres they need.

Similarly, he does not generally buy and sell cars but will occasionally when customers need him to do so as a favour.

Every week, over a mug of tea or coffee, Andy runs an informal team meeting with everyone who works in the garage. They talk about how the week has gone, what went well, and have a no-blame conversation about what didn't go so well. Andy, or anyone else, can raise issues – the implications of impending legislation, technical difficulties with a certain type of repair or how to proactively generate new business.

Andy keeps alert to the learning needs of individuals and talks one-to-one with his people to update their technical and customer relations skills, or to plan how to increase other skills. On the rare occasion that someone leaves he selects staff very carefully, often living with a shortage of staff until he is able to attract the talented person he is looking for. His garage is a happy, challenging and supportive setting in which to work.

It is a small but graphic success story. I will use Andy's garage as long as I'm based in Bristol. I drive Citroëns and Peugeots so that I can use his garage!

Of course we need more than one story to develop a reliable picture of what makes the best organisations stand out from the rest. There are several frameworks and substantial pieces of research evidence to help identify the main ingredients of success. Here we examine two studies showing what excellent organisations have in common and describing quality and excellence awards.

studies of excellent organisations
study 1

The Hambleden Group, a London-based consultancy, studied over 500 companies that had achieved enduring, significant, profitable growth. They termed these companies 'hyper-growth'. All the 'hyper-growth' companies did the following:

■ focused the chief executive officer mainly on influencing stakeholders, eg investors, key customers and suppliers, and employees;
■ clearly defined the role of every employee;
■ trained their people, focusing on training's contribution to business performance;
■ encouraged their people to generate and voice new ideas;
■ empowered managers and staff from the top, so that people know they can take decisions they can justify on behalf of the company.

In addition, Hambleden discovered that most of the 'hyper-growth' companies:

■ compared themselves with competitors and learnt from organisations outside their industry;
■ avoided head-on price confrontation in their markets, eg by differentiating their product or service from that of competitors;
■ exported overseas;
■ marketed collaboratively and formed joint ventures;
■ constantly reduced new product/service development time;
■ used the latest technology;
■ delegated full authority from top to bottom;
■ made acquisitions mainly to obtain new skills;

- included employees in capital growth;
- employed mainly graduate managers;
- employed significantly from outside their industry;
- focused the board on customer service.

study 2

The UK's Department of Trade and Industry collaborated with the Confederation of British Industry to gather the views of the leaders of 121 successful UK-based businesses. Again the aim was to identify the ingredients for success. They concluded that 9 out of 10 winning UK companies:

- are led by visionary, enthusiastic champions of change;
- unlock the potential of their people through:
  - creating a culture in which employees are genuinely empowered and focused on the customer, so that employees are allowed the flexibility to use their own initiative to respond to customer needs;
  - investing in people through good communications, using teams and training to reap the benefits of an informed workforce, working well in their teams and properly trained to do their jobs;
  - flattening and inverting the organisational pyramid so that the workforce is supported rather than controlled to give of their best;
- know their customers through:
  - constantly learning from others;
  - welcoming the challenge of demanding customers to drive innovation and competitiveness;
- constantly introduce new, differentiated products and services – ones that can be presented as different and superior to those of competitors through:
  - developing deep knowledge of their competitors;

- encouraging innovation to successfully exploit new ideas;
- focusing on core businesses complemented by strategic alliances with other organisations;
▓ exceed their customers' expectations with new products and services.

'excellence' frameworks

The US Baldridge Award and its derivatives, for example the Excellence Model developed by the European Foundation for Quality Management and the Australian Quality Award, share a number of criteria believed to contribute to excellence in public and private sector organisations. They recognise the importance of:

▓ leadership;
▓ strategy and planning;
▓ people management;
▓ identifying and attending to key organisational processes.

These generate valued results for:

▓ customers;
▓ employees;
▓ society (in two out of the three frameworks);
▓ the organisation.

The quality models imply that around one-third of organisational success comes from employee-related matters. The models promote the notion that excellence depends in part on how well leaders and managers develop and articulate the organisation's central purposes, and on how they lead and manage employees in the interests of the organisation's stake-holders in general and its customers in particular.

what makes organisations excellent

Drawing the various strands of the studies and the excellence frameworks together we can say that excellence comes from the following:

Having a business or service idea that resonates with stake-holders. Excellent organisations must deliver a substantial benefit valued by those it serves in order to thrive. Consumers, the key stakeholders, will have to like a new flavour of cola before they buy another can, and young people must like coming to a youth centre, and keep on returning to it, for it to remain open. An idea, however well presented, must meet customer needs for the organisation to flourish. In addition other stakeholders must, among other things, value the organi-sation's products if they are to invest time, effort, money or goodwill.

Being clear what the organisation is there to do and what it stands for. Knowing what business it is in, what its mission is, and how it will conduct itself is critical for lasting success. Yes, corrupt, fast-buck companies do exist, but usually not for long. Clarity is as important for a government agency, or even a religious order, as it is for a business.

A public sector adoption agency could perceive itself as being in the business of finding parents for children. It could also, or alternatively, see itself as being in the business of finding chil-dren for prospective parents. These alternatives have very different implications for what the organisation is there to do, what it stands for and how it will need to go about its work. A garage there to help customers take the stress out of owning a car is in a different business to one that sees itself as processing the fixing of cars.

Being clear, and spelling out purpose and direction, is pretty challenging for most organisations. In Chapter 2 we will look at how it can be done, and done in a way that reaps the benefits from appraisal.

Being mindful of the expectations of stakeholders. Stakeholders include investors, customers, employees, suppliers, and the wider society. These stakeholders make different contributions to organisations and expect different returns. The wider community may also have expectations that need to be assessed and addressed.

Excellent organisations can and do map stakeholder requirements, negotiate with stakeholders, track how their expectations are changing and meet the challenge of reconciling the tensions between their various demands. Expectations that the organisation intends to meet should feed their way into the organisation's performance management and performance appraisal process.

Being sensitive to the needs and wants of customers. A government agency responsible for handling the payroll of government employees needs to understand and negotiate its customers' expectations just as much as a supermarket chain. A supermarket chain needs to know how customer requirements are changing. It needs to ask what customers want of a supermarket now, what they will want in a few years' time, and ask itself whether it should be delivering it now. Few organisations will survive, let alone be excellent, if they cannot meet or exceed what the customer wants. No organisation can expect to succeed if it doesn't fulfil its promise to customers. Performance appraisal is one way of helping the organisation fulfil its promise.

Benchmarking against competitors and other organisations.
Let us say that an organisation guarantees to respond to
customer questions within 24 hours, delivers on time in 95 per
cent of instances, has reduced its debtor days by half over the
last three years and has a staff turnover of 40 per cent while
two years ago it was 50 per cent. Is this good, bad or indif-
ferent?

Excellent organisations make it their business to know how
their performance rates against other organisations, seeking
intelligence on how competitors and others operate in order to
improve. Excellent organisations learn by studying the practices of competitors at home and abroad, and they look at what
very different organisations do. A large distribution centre can
learn from how baggage is handled at a major airport. A
specialist up-market chocolate company can learn from a
company selling expensive fountain pens.

Being on top of relevant technology. Hard and soft technology matters to excellent organisations. They keep up to date
on the technologies that are relevant and can benefit their
organisation – eg in IT, CAD/CAM, therapies or the latest
insights into customer behaviour.

Excellent organisations are on top of useful methods of
increasing speed and accuracy, reducing costs and applying
know-how through the application of technology. They are
superb at working out where the technology can and cannot
deliver and are good at spotting false promises as well as
winners.

Knowing where and how to sell. The business of translating
market need into firm, profitable, orders can make or break a
commercial organisation. The principles of sound marketing
and selling also apply to organisations other than businesses.
Excellent organisations of all kinds know how and where to
sell, whether they are successfully run swimming pools, banks,
or make and sell hand-crafted furniture. They know their

target markets and their most likely prospects. They also know how to reach their markets.

Sales people are perceived very differently in different organisations. Excellent organisations see them as heroes. Sales functions are at the core of excellent organisations. Less successful organisations can perceive their sales people as villains, or as a group of people who make unrealistic and fluctuating demands upon the production function.

Managing innovation. The paradox between free-flowing creativity and the discipline of turning ideas into action is handled well by excellent organisations. They know that both are necessary, and know how to do both. Being able constantly to bring new products and services to market quickly pays off. In many sectors it is becoming a key differentiator between the best and the bankrupt.

Excellent organisations are more able than less successful organisations to do old things differently and to do new things. They are usually good at blending the intuition and experience of their people. They use structured processes for bringing about improvement.

Pulling the people management act together. All of the things that make excellent organisations stand out have one thing in common: they depend upon the organisation's people to make them happen. It is quite common for an excellent organisation to be 10 or 12 times as effective as the average performer in their sector. A significant distinctive factor of an excellent organisation is that it has its people management act together.

Using leading edge technology may take money, but it also takes people who are able and enabled to make the right decision as to which technology or equipment to buy.

The ability to balance the needs of customers with those of suppliers is not an innate skill. It takes thought. It also requires sensitivity. People have to have the desire and the capacity to handle their own emotions and those of others. Sales people do not automatically see their job as helping people to buy, rather than as selling them something. However, establishing the former attitude can and must be achieved if the organisation is to be successful over time. In short it takes committed, able, people to do the things that make excellent organisations excellent: not just those at the top, but a critical mass throughout the organisation who are prepared to learn, grow, change and keep on going. Such people do not arrive in an organisation by happy accident. It takes leadership and management to create a workforce that sees a distinct overlap between their own and the organisation's interests.

Not only do excellent organisations know the value of their workforce, they also use practical means to demonstrate that they value them. They are concerned to mine the talent that is available by:

■ Getting recruitment, retention and day-to-day management right most of the time.

■ Using organisational politics as a strength. They use power constructively to manoeuvre people into situations where they confront problems, resolve difficulties and are prepared to change.

■ Managing employee performance in harmony with the management of the organisation's performance, in order to support the organisation's purpose and direction.

■ Keeping in touch with the demands and expectations of employees. They are vigilant in checking that people-management policies and practices are delivering what they should and could deliver.

■ Sustaining a climate where people are prepared to give of their best and then to improve upon their best. In these settings employees are ready to adapt, changing even well-entrenched and treasured ways of working which they are able to recognise no longer suits the context within which the organisation operates.

The performance of people is critical. Excellent organisations know that it is too important to be left unmanaged. They set about managing performance in a planned and conscious way.

managing performance

Some organisations seem to have an effortless practice of managing performance to lead to success. Those organisations with effective performance management have developed a clear idea about what they realistically can and want to achieve. This clarity has allowed them to focus on a small number of things they must do really well if they are not only to survive, but thrive and achieve their goals. They use a carefully selected set of measures to collect data which really does tell them how they are doing. The information is 'hard' and 'soft'. Successful organisations, whether they are companies or public sector service providers, know, for example, that the feelings and perceptions of customers and services users are just as important as the figures.

While managing performance, they know how to keep on improving their activities in the light of what is happening in the marketplace and other parts of the world that are important to them. Successful organisations know how to acquire and retain the resources they need, and know how to focus the use of those resources.

As well as remaining focused on what they want to achieve and checking their progress, they are alert to changes in the marketplace which may call for adjustments to their focus. Their leaders and managers have the capacity to listen to the people in their teams, and channel relevant information in such a way as to energise teams and individuals. This allows teams to collaborate with, support, learn from, and constructively challenge other individuals and teams.

Successful organisations will not do all these things perfectly, of course. But they know that in order to tip the balance in their favour all they need is to do things just that little bit better than their competitors or comparable organisations. For some organisations it is as simple as this. No need for grand theories, no frills and, heaven forbid, maybe no need for management consultants!

Many successful organisations know that all it takes is for people in the organisation to be doing the common sense, the simple, things exceptionally well. But that can, of course, be asking a lot of some people and some organisations. Some if not most organisations need some structures and processes to discipline the management of performance at organisation level, team level and at the level of the individual.

It is easy to lose sight of the organisation's central purposes, become diverted by the latest crisis, fad or seductive business or service opportunity that is interesting, new, but *slightly* off-beam.

It is also seductive to believe that if the organisation has a performance management process, incorporating an appraisal process, then it will necessarily deliver success. Reasons other than successful performance management can account for an organisation's success. For one thing, there might be no competition. The organisation will remain successful until 'me-too' competitors emerge, who can mimic the product or service, particularly if the competitors turn out to be more efficient. Others who, while successful, do not manage their people particularly well are vulnerable to competitors who are brushing up their performance management act. Performance management is not a *sine qua non* for success. What it can do is make the difference, when all other things are apparently equal. Imagine a race with identical horses and identical jockeys: the horse whose performance has been managed so that it pushes its nose in front at the finishing line is that one that wins.

showing that performance matters

My experience working with clients and reading the research and the literature suggests that seven pillars of performance management need to be in place to contribute to an organisation being excellent. These are:

▓ **Clarity about the organisation's purpose and direction** expressed in language that people and teams at different levels can understand.

▓ **Clear understanding by individuals and teams** about what they are expected to do and deliver, ie which bit of the organisational jigsaw they represent.

▓ **Aspiration:** mechanisms to help people recognise that continuous improvement is essential, not just desirable, and to know what excellent performance looks like.

▓ **Support:** mechanisms to encourage and support performance, enabling individuals to have the self-confidence to recognise their own potential and training needs; supervisors and managers who know how to motivate their people and are able to coach.

▓ **Feedback loops** so that people and teams know how they are doing against the expectations: this is where *appraisal* fits in as well as less structured ongoing day-to-day feedback from managers, colleagues, customers.

▓ **Recognition:** ways of rewarding and recognising people that are not all about pay.

▓ **Renewal:** the energy and enthusiasm to start all over again because the other six features have proved valuable to those involved.

After 30 years in management education, management development and consultancy it's clear to me that appraisal processes fail or under-deliver mainly because organisations try to build appraisal systems with only a few of these seven pillars in place. Without the support of all seven pillars, the structure is doomed quickly to deteriorate.

Chapter 3 deals in detail with mistaken practices and approaches to appraisal. The key point is that without surrounding people *and their managers* with the message that performance matters, appraisal will disappoint. In the next few chapters we will explore what can be done to surround people with the message that performance matters, concentrating mainly on performance appraisal itself. We will also look at other aspects of performance management that feed into and reinforce the goals of appraisal processes.

preconditions to appraisal contributing to excellence

Performance appraisal processes only operate effectively if certain preconditions are met.

scene-setting
what needs to be clear?

Would you want to get on a train if you didn't know where it was going? If so, would you get excited about it?

Well, maybe yes, maybe no. Mystery tours have their attractions, but to take one every day might be too much of a good thing. Most people are interested in having some idea of where they are going.

Even though many people just want 'a job', they are more likely to feel more fulfilled working somewhere they can see, and have sympathy with, what the organisation is doing. They want to know what the organisation is setting out to achieve, both in the short and longer term. They appreciate transparency, and given the choice, usually prefer to identify with the organisation.

My work with organisations that are operating below their potential suggests that many of their leaders and managers do not want to clarify their organisation's purpose and where it is heading. These management teams tend to work in one of two ways.

They assume that the mission and direction are obvious and believe there is no point in articulating the organisation's aspirations. Alternatively, they draw up vision and mission statements, values statements and so on in something of a hurry, as an exercise, and then publish them to impress various audiences – shareholders, banks, some government inspectorate. Then they carry on running the organisation as though these efforts to clarify their purpose and direction are irrelevant.

Wiser heads are much more circumspect about the task of clarifying and occasionally re-clarifying what the organisation is about, and what excellence means to the organisation. They play around, purposefully, with the words they use, so that through the process of debate they reach a consensus. Having achieved that consensus they are then in a position to bring it to life by communicating it to all the people in the organisation.

Naturally, good managers and leaders find ways of genuinely involving their people in developing the consensus. Usually they select areas where employees can and do make helpful contributions, and thereby avoid being accused of phoney consultation.

vision, mission, values

People need to know the organisation's vision, mission and values, especially those that differentiate it from other apparently similar organisations. It means making a statement about what makes a particular school, drinks company, legal firm or software house distinctive. Even very similar organisations have some characteristics that could make them stand out in employees' minds from the rest. For example, a search on the Web sites of British Airways and KLM will show that the former has a mission to be 'the undisputed leader in world travel' while the latter aspires to 'participate in one of the leading global airline systems'. KLM aims to 'provide a stimulating and stable working environment for its employees' while British Airways wants to be 'team spirited'.

I will avoid fine-tuned working definitions of the concepts of vision, mission and organisational values. It is sufficient to say that what people need to be clear about are the central purposes of an organisation, where it is heading, and how it wants to go about its business. Clarity also increases when employees are helped to understand what the organisation is *not* about and for whom it is not catering.

Here are some examples of how a few organisations across the world express what they are about:

a charitable organisation in Canada
The Arnprior & District Archives is a multi-municipal institution established by local volunteers as a non-profit charitable organisation, serving the citizens of the Town of Arnprior and McNab/Braeside Township. The Archives was established to acquire, preserve and make accessible important historical documents pertaining to the history of the area.

the University of California Police Department
The University of California Police Department at Los Angeles is a leader in providing progressive law enforcement services to a culturally diverse urban campus and its surrounding community. We actively foster a safe environment by maintaining a high state of readiness, cultivating community partnerships, and creating innovative community programs.

a cat club
The Southern British Shorthair Cat Club is a Breed Club for British Shorthair Cats, specifically formed to serve the needs of breeders and enthusiasts located in the South of England. (Note that it does not appear to want to cater for cat breeders and enthusiasts outside the South of England.)

Xerox
Xerox Mission Statement
Our strategic intent is to be the leader in the global document market, providing document solutions that enhance business productivity.

Xerox Values
Since our inception, we have operated under the guidance of six core values:

1. We succeed through satisfied customers.
2. We value and empower employees.
3. We deliver quality and excellence in all we do.
4. We provide superior return to our shareholders.
5. We use technology to deliver market leadership.
6. We behave responsibly as a corporate citizen.

Less wordy statements also help. I understand that 'Beat Coke!' and 'Let's get Porsche!' are used in two major international companies.

creating clarity
The challenge for leaders is to translate the statements of corporate purpose and values into something that enlivens and inspires people. Managers need to *create* clarity and meaning for their people. Writing the values down, or even reciting them as a mantra, will not necessarily bring about the behaviour required to make the values manifest. Neither will just providing people with a list of tasks.

In retail outlets, for example, enthusing checkout staff to make customers feel welcome and talking through the significance of doing so produces greater clarity than simply instructing someone to smile at least three times during the customer's stop at the checkout. Communicating the 'what' sufficiently clearly so that staff can and want to take on some of the responsibility for deciding on the 'how' is likely to produce more effective realisation of the vision than denying staff the opportunity to respond to the vision in their own way.

In short it takes leadership *and* management to produce clarity of purpose, direction and values. This theme is picked up by John Kotter in his book *A Force for Change: How leadership differs from management*. Kotter helpfully distinguishes between the preoccupations of leaders and managers.

His research concludes that *managers* are concerned with planning and budgeting, organising and staffing, controlling and problem solving, and producing a degree of predictability and order. *Leaders*, on the other hand, concern themselves with establishing direction, aligning people in cooperative relationships, motivating and inspiring and producing change.

Clarifying, through meaningful statements of vision, mission and values, is about *leading*. Reinforcing these statements relies on good leadership *and* really good *management* so that the key messages are reinforced daily.

commitment to improvement

One of my clients once startled her complacent, conservative and change-averse board members by saying, 'We don't have to get any better at what we are doing… [long pause]… but survival isn't compulsory either'.

Complacency is the death of ambition. If organisations have lost ambition then they are resigning themselves to, at best, getting by, or at worst, looking at ways of sliding into decline.

Once standards of performance are articulated and owned, some performance improvements can seem effortless. They happen spontaneously, incrementally, and instinctively. Where there is a substantial need for improvement the individual improvements need to be consciously and deliberately planned. Improvement sometimes needs the structure of suitable improvement tools and techniques. Total Quality Management tools and techniques and those found in programmes such as the Profit from Innovation programme (see Chapter 4) help to identify what needs to be improved and how to bring about the improvement. Improvements need to be prioritised. Decisions concerning priorities will be helped by reference to the organisation's key purposes.

The principal of a college announced that the improvements the college was looking for fell into three categories:

■ those that helped the college increase the number of students;
■ those that helped students successfully to complete their programmes;
■ those that reduced costs while retaining quality.

This approach underlined key goals and gave shape to the improvement plan.

However clear and focused the plan for improvement, it may feel like unacceptable change to anyone who isn't clear about the reasons for it, and the implications for their own position. Managing change effectively means leaders and managers being ready to engage in a dialogue about:

■ where the change will take the organisation;
■ why it is a good idea;
■ the implications of change for individuals.

Introducing change is particularly demanding for leaders and managers when they themselves are uncomfortable or resistant to it. They need to be able to handle their own feelings while still providing clarity for others. There is a substantial literature and on-the-ground experience on this topic. It suffices to say here that uncertainty about change consumes an enormous amount of time and energy through unhelpful anxiety, gossip and speculation.

The more secretive the organisation, the more it massages the truth and misleads people, the more employees become clear about one thing: the organisation and its managers cannot be trusted. This is not the sort of clarity we are after!

expressing expectations

Typically, organisations describe:

- what the individual needs to bring to the job or learn to be able to do, eg current competencies and those they need to acquire;
- the contribution their jobs are meant to make, eg through a role description, broad key result areas;
- what they are meant to do, eg through a job description;
- what they are meant to achieve, eg through articulating measurable targets and measurable objectives;
- the attitudes and values that are helpful to the organisation, eg through codes of conduct.

These expectations are formally written down, orally presented as a formal set-piece and then reinforced (or contradicted) through what is said and done day-to-day. The power of what happens day-to-day should not be underestimated. What managers, colleagues, customers and suppliers say and do shapes the individual's picture of what is expected. Old-style quality inspectors will know the pressure they experience to 'let things through' when there is pressure to meet customer volume requirements. Social workers and others in the caring professions may feel pressure to decide against certain actions when budgets are stretched.

Sometimes the most powerful thing the individual or individual's manager can do is to recognise when the individual's behaviour is being shaped in ways that do not line up with that intended, for example when formal and informal ground rules contradict each other. Identifying such difficulties does, of course, require regular and sensitive contact so that the individual and his or her manager can work together to sharpen up the picture of expectations. Although there are mechanisms for letting people know what is expected of them the mechanisms are not guaranteed to 'work' without a fair amount of energy being expended in checking the impact of immediate demands on the stated aims of the organisation.

what supports performance?

The support to acquire and hold on to the picture of what is expected is one of many facilities the organisation can provide to generate effective performance. Other forms of support are important too.

It is very important to finds ways of enabling individuals to have the confidence to operate without patronising them. A mother returning to work after successfully raising four children needs few lessons in practical logistics and time management, but she may still need help to transfer those skills to a new setting.

To have an entire organisation's people saying realistically, 'Yes, I can do that', is a big prize. To have all people say '... and I want to do it and will do it well' is an even bigger prize.

In any organisation there will be those whose performance affects others' ability to do their job. Supervisors and managers need to lead and manage both those reporting to them and the key people who impact on their performance to ensure that each person operates as an energy giver and not an energy sapper.

Frank Hartle's book on performance management and Mike Dutfield and Chris Eling's book on managers' communication consider what effective managers have to do to create a climate where people are motivated to give of their best. What effective managers do is to:

- spell out what is expected of people by expressing expectations through measurable objectives where possible and helping people identify the competencies the job or task needs;
- actively listen to people and support them to share information and ideas through using eliciting skills;
- communicate with people through using a repertoire of presentation skills;
- help people learn on-the-job and near-the-job through coaching and by deliberately providing new experiences;
- advise on performance improvements;
- recognise and reinforce good performance;
- identify and challenge unacceptable performance.

As we will see later, a sound approach to performance appraisal pays off because it provides a forum where good, skilful, managers can exercise some or all of these competencies to good effect.

what does excellence look like?

People need to know what excellence in their organisation looks like in practice. They need broad statements of vision, mission and values to be turned into something concrete which makes sense to them. What makes sense can vary dramatically from job to job and individual to individual. For example, detailed performance figures that will interest institutional investors may do little to galvanise the actions of employees. The challenge to leaders is to decide which standards of performance are critical to the organisation and then to find ways of making employees identify with and seek to deliver or exceed those standards.

One of my clients made a breakthrough in promoting the significance of meeting high levels of product reliability via newsletters, team talks and the organisation's induction/orientation programme. His company operated in the elevator business, and his message was simple: 'If one of our installations fails badly there is a one in five chance of someone dying'.

Another organisation I worked with is established in the youth and social work field. One of the agency's hostels houses young men, many of whom have a prison record. They treat institutions with suspicion. During a staff meeting the agency's Director summed up the hostel and what it was trying to achieve by saying: 'The hostel is here to provide residents with a second chance. We have to be at our very best because they may only give us one chance to help them'.

But just describing standards of performance that people can easily relate to is not enough. It is relatively easy to achieve this where there is a ready emotional appeal. It is just as important, but a great deal harder to achieve, when emotive means cannot be used. The real skill is making the unexciting exciting and significant. This needs an unusual combination of flair, seriousness and drama. And when that isn't available in the organisation, it needs to be imported or developed.

There are substantial rewards to be won from the organisation knowing and being clear about what to strive for. It then becomes possible for people at all levels of the organisation to know what excellent organisational performance looks like. In turn it becomes possible for people to acknowledge and accept what they need to deliver. Finally, it becomes easier to identify what needs to be improved and how everyone can contribute to the improvement.

getting it wrong

when appraisal becomes a lungfish

The West African lungfish, *proptopterus annectens*, seems able to sense the onset of the dry season, burrows into the mud or clay and secretes a mucous cocoon around itself before the water it usually lives in evaporates. A small vent in the cocoon allows the dormant fish to breathe and it can stay alive for three to four years without water. When the rains come the cocoon softens and the fish can live in the water again. If the rains do not come for three or four years, the fish dies. I have met a few lungfish appraisal processes in my time.

There can be great activity and promise on their introduction: working groups are involved in design, consultants are engaged, and forms and manuals are produced. There is much agonising about establishing clear boundaries between appraisal and disciplinary mechanisms, and fierce battles are fought over the calibration of measurement instruments. Consultants are brought in to sprinkle holy water on the process and to pray that it will work. Finally, after much agonising as to whether the process should be related to remuneration and after briefing and training of staff and managers the scheme is launched. For a while there is a flurry of activity and much shuffling of paper. Then there is a quiet period, sometimes as long as three to four years. Finally an HR person, rarely the chief executive, pronounces that:

■ the process is moribund;
■ only 40 per cent of managers are completing the required paperwork and even fewer are holding face-to-face appraisal discussions that are valued by the appraisee;
■ corporate training plans cannot be drawn up based on the output;
■ some good people are leaving because they cannot trust the organisation to take a genuine interest in their development and career.

A meeting is called to decide whether the rain is going to be allowed to soften the cocoon and a genuine attempt made to change the prevailing climate. The decision may be to announce the death of the process and move on to the next people management panacea: coaching, leadership training, quality circles or updating job descriptions using a new format.

What can reinvigorate the lungfish is an insistence that the appraisal process be firmly connected to the rest of the organisation's performance management and people management processes. Either that, or the honesty and courage to accept that there are insufficient robust people management and performance management policies and practices in place for the organisation to contemplate the introduction of an appraisal process.

There is a temptation to cut corners, to try to pursue appraisal without the infrastructure alluded to in Chapter 1. It is critical for key connections to be in place. Some of the activities that preceded the death of the lungfish are necessary: boundaries between appraisal and other processes do need to be clarified, for example. But much more needs to be connected.

An appraisal process can survive for a while in isolation, but it will eventually degenerate if it is not connected to other performance management processes, nor sustained by the fundamental processes sustaining the organisation. *Dis*connection might look like this:

▧ launching appraisal as a stand-alone process with no link to any other performance management practices, eg to organisational performance objectives, career management, or a competency framework;

▧ excusing senior managers from any responsibility or accountability for designing the appraisal process, deeming it an HR department problem;

▧ determining investment in training and development without any reference to the appraisal process or the organisation's priorities;

▧ confusing the boundary between appraisal and the disciplinary procedure;

▧ failing to set up monitoring of the conduct or contribution of the process;

▧ failing to discuss the appraisee's career aspirations in the interview or subsequently because appraisers are too busy coping with the short term.

The rest of this book helps readers to set up and use appraisal as a key performance management tool so that performance appraisal becomes constructive, meaningful and even enjoyable.

useful lessons

As a consultant I have frequently been engaged to revive lungfish in danger of expiring. In this revivalist role I have unearthed several practices that undermine the possibility of performance appraisal working for the organisation and have witnessed all of the following:

Sending the message that the organisation's management is not committed to appraisal:

- letting it be known that the chief executive is not appraised, or has his or her appraisal over a leisurely dinner with the least demanding board member;
- delegating the design of the appraisal process to one or two of the least able and most authoritarian of middle managers;
- ensuring that the process only covers some key groups of staff so that people who are not included feel even more marginalised;
- announcing a reduction in the training budget at the start of an appraisal 'season' or at the introduction of a process or redesigned process.

Building tension and anxiety into a new or revised appraisal process:

- adopting the 'Mafia model': letting it be known that the process will encourage judgements to be made on personal characteristics, initiative, loyalty, etc, and that the results of these evaluations will not be discussed with the individual but will be acted upon;
- publishing guidelines that all appraisal documentation and discussion should follow an identical format without reference to the preferences of the appraiser or appraisee and without taking into account the nature of the job, or alternatively leaving the format entirely up to the appraiser and his or her idiosyncrasies;
- publicly asking appraisers to make copious notes of all points made by the appraisee so that the information will be extremely useful when considering who to 'let go' in the next reorganisation;
- not agreeing in advance a date and time for the appraisal discussion, but springing the appraisal on the person;

▨ not training appraisers or appraisees, or providing appraisees with little or no briefing but running two-day or three-day training courses for appraisers.

Compromising the process design:

▨ overloading the process with multiple functions all of which have to be covered in a short discussion, eg an assessment of performance, a career discussion, making the process a test-bed for performance-related pay, a training needs analysis, target setting, semi-disciplinary counselling and work planning;

▨ calling any face-to-face meeting an 'interview', thus emphasising the imbalance in the relationship between appraiser and appraisee;

▨ making it obvious that spotting serious weaknesses is a major goal;

▨ prohibiting a preparatory meeting to agree specific aims for the appraisal and the appraisal discussion with the individual;

▨ designing a minimalist approach in order to go through the motions, eg because the parent company wants 'a scheme' introduced;

▨ excluding middle managers, who will be important appraisers, from the design of the appraisal process and presenting it to them as a non-negotiable *fait accompli.*

Conducting appraisal 'interviews' that alarm all but the totally insensitive:

▨ spending the whole of the meeting searching for and anticipating problems and weaknesses, in the belief that the appraisee's strengths are already known;

▨ not discussing any achievements, presuming that these will have been obvious to the appraisee when they occurred;

- conducting the meeting in a place and in a way that makes it clear that there is no commitment to promised privacy and confidentiality;
- ostensibly in the interest of efficiency, recording the interview directly on to a laptop computer, placing the machine so that the appraisee cannot see what is being recorded and has to peer over the screen to speak to the appraiser;
- not taking notes, so that when the time comes to write up the meeting, several weeks later, the appraiser will only be able to record a few sketchy comments;
- not producing the notes of the meeting, even though this was promised;
- fitting three or four appraisal meetings into an hour with a watch placed on the desk;
- not establishing a ground rule of no interruptions during appraisal discussions;
- manipulating the appraisee to agree to unrealistic plans even when the appraiser knows they are unrealistic;
- criticising the appraisee for not delivering things over which he or she has no control or for not working towards objectives that were not previously established;
- not listening to the appraisee;
- ignoring any notes or papers the appraisee has brought with him or her by way of preparation;
- making promises the appraiser and/or appraisee know cannot be kept;
- making promises to the appraisee on behalf of other people without checking out their readiness to comply;
- refusing to discuss the appraiser's career aspirations in the appraisal discussion and refusing to set up another meeting to discuss it – the appraiser is too busy coping with the short term.

I promise that these things have all happened! They are dysfunctional because the appraisal process is carrying the burden of, rather than being supported by, the seven pillars of performance management listed in Chapter 1 and because the handling of the appraisal discussion is seriously flawed. When faced with some of these dysfunctions here is what happens:

Christine had worked for nine months as a middle manager for a well-known, moderately successful financial service organisation. She had a reputation as a good manager, focused on results and good with people. She was due to appraise Mark, one of her staff.

Because her predecessor, Brian, had not agreed performance targets at the last appraisal, Christine had met Mark to agree some targets around three months after she had joined. Mark had been doing well on most targets and Christine had congratulated him as the opportunity arose.

When Mark came into her room she and he sat across the corner of a table. As the appraisal discussion progressed, Mark, although usually responsive, said very little and was tense. Christine had great difficulty in encouraging him to engage in a dialogue. She worked through her agenda that followed a useful framework developed by the HR department. She took notes as she went but was careful to agree them with Mark.

After around an hour Christine smiled at Mark, closed the file, put her pen away and drew her chair back. Despite the 'it's over' signs Mark sat in his chair... and waited.

After several seconds of uncomfortable silence Christine asked, 'Mark, is there anything else you'd like to talk about?' 'It's just that I was waiting for you to tell me what you really thought,' Mark responded.

It transpired that Brian used to run appraisal meetings 'by the book'. However, on completing what for him was the HR ritual he would put the papers away and switch into telling Mark, and other appraisees, about their deficiencies, how they didn't understand the pressure Brian was under, how he doubted that the company had a future and so on.

This is a dismal picture, but not that extreme. Many managers and appraisees learn to 'play the game' and distort the process because they do not think they can benefit from it. It is important that those designing appraisal processes learn from the mistaken practices and approaches described in this chapter.

thinking about appraisal – four foundation issues

Many appraisal processes fail because those responsible for getting them off the ground do not think through what they are doing. They copy another organisation's scheme, without necessarily finding out what it offers its host. Some start by designing forms and then design a process to get the forms completed. Some base the process on job descriptions, often out of date, or on badly conceived objectives or inadequately developed competencies.

Appraisal processes need to be as simple as possible but as complex as necessary. They should not be simplistic.

Figure 4.1 presents a framework for thinking about the design and implementation of performance appraisal.

Even though Figure 4.1 suggests a sequence, those designing appraisal processes will need to go backwards at times before continuing the 10 issues presented: progression will be iterative not linear. For example, the first training session on the intro-duction or relaunch of appraisal usually brings up appraisal process policy and design issues which have not been resolved

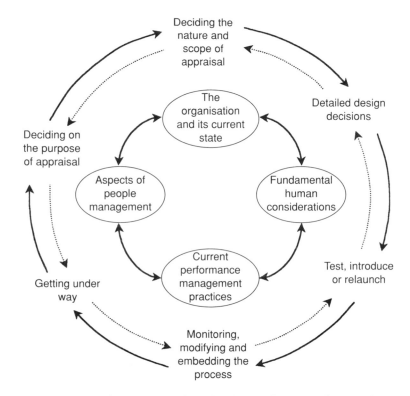

Figure 4.1 *A framework for thinking about and introducing an appraisal process*

in advance; it is unlikely that the design stage will result in a process that has every angle covered.

This chapter considers in detail the four issues in the centre of Figure 4.1. These can make the difference between an appraisal system that contributes to improving and maintaining performance and one that does not. They cannot be ignored. My experience suggests that it need not take a tremendous amount of energy to achieve an effective appraisal process, but there are no short cuts. It is as much about will as it is about skill.

current state of play

A construction company, an airline and a social care organisation operate in different ways and in different environments. It is not possible for a 'one size fits all' appraisal process to work in them all. The complexion of an organisation is made up of many factors, such as the skill and educational levels of employees, employee turnover, the organisation's core 'business', and its size.

employees

In the late 1960s many managers favoured having different processes for different staff. Processes for appraising managers were different from those for technical and administrative employees and different again for manual or shop-floor workers. In the 1970s and 80s I noticed managers switching to a belief in one inclusive scheme. Current practice suggests that the 'one size fits all' process is again being questioned: a professional workforce of engineers, medics or lawyers presents a different challenge to those designing the appraisal process from a workforce of semi-skilled employees.

Different employees respond very differently to appraisal. I know a working group, composed largely of electronics engineers, who spent over an hour arguing fruitlessly about whether to use a five- or six-point scale to measure one aspect of performance. In another organisation, staff accepted with enthusiasm the opportunity for a conversation about performance. They had few concerns about how the process should run. A deep understanding of the organisation and how its people might think about and react to appraisal is essential to designing, introducing or changing an appraisal process to meet the needs of that organisation.

relevance of an appraisal process

Any organisation needs to consider the relevance of an appraisal process to its short- and medium-term outlook. For organisations in deep trouble the introduction of an appraisal process is unlikely to be a top priority. If the organisation has unacceptably high staff turnover, the causes need to be understood before judging whether appraisal will help. Organisations undergoing major changes in reporting relationships need to settle a little before appraisal can contribute. However, when some stability emerges, the introduction of appraisal can help appraiser and appraisee develop mutual understanding of each other's roles and establish a foundation for high performance.

The timing of the introduction in the grand scheme of things needs to 'feel right'. For the process designer it may sometimes be difficult to distinguish between sound, valid reasons, and excuses presented to mask some other, less politically acceptable reasons for undermining the introduction of appraisal.

For the process to have a chance of operating, there needs to be a 'critical mass' of people, particularly at middle-management level, who agree that the introduction of appraisal will take the organisation forward, even if they agree for different reasons.

taking appraisal seriously

Even if the organisation's position can be enhanced by introducing an appraisal process, there may be a significant number of people expressing doubts or hostility. In this case, there are two options. The first is to plough on regardless and hope that there is sufficient goodwill to give appraisal a try and let people be convinced by the resulting benefits. The difficulty with this is that there needs to be sufficient commitment at the right level for the benefits to be experienced. Otherwise, those who are forecasting that appraisal is not worthwhile are the very people being asked to prove that it is. The second option is to expose the doubts or hostility and see if there is a way of dealing with them.

When the signals to go ahead or to wait are not easy to read, managers charged with introducing appraisal are confronted with the dilemma of pressing ahead, chancing success or failure, or opening up debate and risking finding some substantial difficulties. A conflict over introduction might be intractable, for example when a chief executive disinclined to listen to the case against appraisal still demands that an appraisal process be introduced.

organisational structure

Conventional functional hierarchies with several layers present different possibilities and challenges from those that are much flatter. Alternatives to functionally based organisations are increasingly common, for example organisations made of up multifunctional mini-organisations, or project and matrix organisations.

The structure of an organisation affects the ratio of managers to managed, the number of direct reports a manager has and even the extent to which individuals believe they have 'a boss'. The structure gives a particular 'feel' to an organisation and to beliefs about what it takes to make it operate successfully.

organisational culture

Whether an organisation will be receptive to introducing an appraisal process, and if so whether a particular approach will be acceptable, is shaped by its culture. The strong interrelationship between beliefs, values and norms, often unconscious, acts as a traffic light for appraisal processes.

An organisation's culture signals the extent to which a particular approach to performance appraisal will be accepted or rejected. There may be good reason for introducing an approach that tries to shift the beliefs and values underpinning the culture, but it would be reckless to introduce a system without taking the prevailing culture into account in the first place. It would be wise to prepare for and find ways of countering the 'dynamic conservatism' which may be unleashed if there is an attempt to introduce a process deemed to be a bad fit. Many a manager and HR specialist has been very surprised at the blocks placed in the way of introducing or modifying an appraisal process. Blocks stemming from the organisation's culture are difficult and sometimes even impossible to remove. In such circumstances, carrying on regardless of the obstacles may be the only, albeit high-risk, strategy available.

There is a substantial literature on culture, the effect it has on attempts to introduce change, and how culture can or cannot be modified in a short time. We will look at the work of Frank Hartle on work cultures (as shown in Figure 4.2) and Sethia and Von Glinow's work on HR cultures.

Figure 4.2 *Organisation work cultures and their impact on the appraisal of individuals*

Culture and major contributor to appraisal	What seems natural and helpful to appraise	What will feel strange and discordant
Functional work culture – Emphasis on reliability and use of the organisation's core technology through the organisation's functions	Functional competence – as a specialist eg in production, accounting, buying	High value attached to teamwork placing very high emphasis on extent to which individual is a team player in cross-functional teams
Many large manufacturing companies and large areas of both local and central government are good examples	Ability to use logical/analytical thinking Performance against known individual job objectives	Focus on competencies that are underpinned by divergent thinking
Major contributor to appraisal – functional boss and/or boss' boss in function	Ability to persuade other functions Developing a sense of order	Loose, barely structured or 'blank-sheet' appraisal processes
	Developing others, usually within function	

Culture and major contributor to appraisal	What seems natural and helpful to appraise	What will feel strange and discordant
Process work culture – Emphasis towards customer focus with reliability as a major requirement

Reliance on multi-functional teams focusing on customer segments eg in financial services and retail. The organisation 'works backwards' by concentrating design of the organisation and its constituent processes around what is to be delivered and experienced by the customer

Major contributor to appraisal – team leader plus others inside and outside the team, including some outside the organisation eg customers | Specific skills related to process

Extent to which he/she is a team player

Competencies

Skills

Outputs

Flexibility of response within role, rather than job

Contribution to improving process | Ability to stick to the rules

Ability to work alone

Appraisal processes that are all about inputs eg narrow competencies, with no attention to individual's outputs |
| **Time-based work culture** – Emphasis on capitalising on capability/technology and flexibility. Intent on leading their market through doing things better and faster

Computer software companies, 'fashion' companies of various kinds and internal product/ service development teams inside organisations are examples | Contribution to achieving project milestones

Impact on others

Initiative

Creativity/conceptual thinking

Readiness to learn and adapt | Developing solid functional skill

Highly elaborate, time-consuming appraisal processes |

(Figure 4.2 continued.)

Culture and major contributor to appraisal	What seems natural and helpful to appraise	What will feel strange and discordant
Major contributor to appraisal – team leader or leaders, colleagues, credible assessor of technical ability		
Network work culture – Emphasis on flexibility and customers. Bring together people with different expertise in teams, which are often temporary Highly goal-oriented and adaptive. Winners are leading-edge organisations Film companies, consultancies and product promotion companies are examples	Extent to which person contributed to or introduced new ideas or methods Justified self-confidence Team-working skills Relationship building Contribution to delivery Extent to which competencies are consistently improved	Just having an appraisal process, especially one for individuals, may seem odd for some network cultures Complex appraisal processes that address anything other than key competencies and what individual deliver to team effort
Major contributor to appraisal – project leader and colleagues, if still around; customer, if interested		

(Figure 4.2 continued.)

The key point is that in order to have an appraisal process that helps an organisation to operate and to be excellent, the work culture has to be taken into account. It is not about being defeated by it at first base. However, it is about being clear about the nature and size of the obstacles placed in the way of appraisal.

If sifting the evidence makes it clear that resistance will be insurmountable and that the culture will spit out the appraisal process, then there is some hard thinking to do before going ahead. There may be some battles to challenge and change the culture. Introducing a performance appraisal process is un-likely by itself to change an organisation's culture, but as one of several interventions, it may make a contribution to culture change.

Sethia and Von Glinow provide a typology of HR cultures, suggesting two dimensions to plot them: 'concern for people' and 'concern for performance'. 'Concern for people' refers to the extent to which an organisation respects individual dignity and is committed to employees' well-being. 'Concern for performance' represents the extent to which the organisation expects that employees 'will do their best on their jobs and make full use of their talents'. Figure 4.3 presents the typology of four cultures that can be identified by plotting where an organisation registers on the two dimensions. This provides appraisal designers with a sketch map to help them position their efforts to introduce or modify an appraisal process.

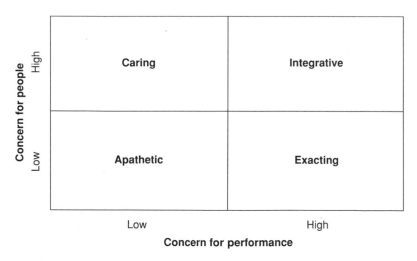

'Arriving at Four Cultures', by Nirmal K. Sethia & Mary Ann Von Glinow in *Gaining Control of the Corporate Culture*, Ralph H. Kilmann *et al*. Copyright Jossey-Bass. Reprinted by permission of Jossey-Bass Inc., a subsidiary of John Wiley & Sons Inc.

Figure 4.3   *A framework of HR culture*

Sethia and Von Glinow stress that the typology does not commend a 'best' culture. The culture may be, or may have been, an appropriate or understandable response to an organisation's past environment. We can now consider the key characteristics of each culture and the implications they have for appraisal.

An Apathetic HR culture:

■ Shows low concern for people as people and for how well they do their jobs. Some of the pre-privatised utilities in the UK would have been in this category.

■ Is unlikely to have performance appraisal processes or performance management in general. If processes are in place, they will have little to do with concern for employees or their performance, but will reflect a concern to *appear* interested in both, perhaps to please external stakeholders.

Attempting to change this HR culture by introducing appraisal is unlikely to generate a shift to a more acceptable culture without other, more influential, interventions.

A Caring HR culture:

■ Places strong emphasis on concern for people, supported through recognisable mechanisms or systems to support them.

■ May well have performance appraisal in place, perhaps not called 'appraisal' but 'development discussion', 'development planning or 'career review'.

■ Will *not* involve placing high standards of performance on employees.

■ Will be essentially paternalistic.

■ Will take care not to overtax people. If people want to drive themselves, that is up to them, but the appraisal will pay little or no attention to eliciting high performance on behalf of customers.

Intervening to change this culture rapidly by introducing performance appraisal that shifts attention away from a concern for the individual towards a concern for performance is likely to be strongly resisted, by managers as well as rank-and-file employees.

An Exacting HR culture:

■ Demands high performance irrespective of an individual's personal or domestic circumstances.

■ May have hard-edged performance management and appraisal processes, in extreme cases based on a hard-nosed management-by-objectives process only.

■ Places emphasis on the extent to which employees, in particular managers, are delivering what they promised.

■ Pays little regard to the fact that the targets and measurements agreed at the start of the appraisal period may have become much more difficult to achieve. Loose objectives will be tightened up significantly.

■ Makes the setting and revision of objectives vital and anxiety-ridden, especially for the appraisee.

This is the exact opposite of the Caring HR culture. It is not surprising that in this culture the part of some performance appraisal processes which asks employees to commit to what they will deliver during the appraisal period have been dubbed 'suicide kits'. In this culture, employees who are off-target would be wise to look for good career and outplacement consultants.

A shift from a Caring culture to an Exacting culture, although difficult to achieve, might be appropriate if there is a concern to underline that the nature of the organisation is changing.

An Integrative HR culture:

▓ Places strong emphasis on concern for people *and* concern for their performance. This concern is not driven by paternalism but from a genuine respect for people and their capacity to learn, grow and contribute.

▓ Places strong emphasis on performance stimulated by the organisation's response to its market and competitive environment.

▓ Has performance management and appraisal processes which place similar weightings on performance objectives, targets and so on as on learning, eg through training and development. In this culture there are genuine attempts to weave emphasis on people and on their performance into the day-to-day life of the organisation.

Attempts to shift the emphasis more towards one dimension than another may be vigorously resisted. This may happen even if the organisation's environment is signalling the need to make such shifts; for example when the existence of highly predatory competitors requires a 'toughening-up' on the performance dimension.

In the unlikely circumstance of an organisation with an Integrative culture not having formal performance management and performance appraisal, their introduction, sensitively handled, would not be difficult. Any resistance is likely to come from managers and employees concerned that formalising the processes may reduce their impact. Their fear is that making the process more transparent may weaken, rather than strengthen, the organisation's approach to appraisal: by making the organisation's way of doing things so obvious, people may feel awkward and uncomfortable as 'natural' behaviour is formalised.

current approach and previous experience

Imagine the following scenarios:

▨ An organisation already has an appraisal process but it is flawed in some way or deemed to be under-delivering.

▨ An organisation does not have an existing process and has little by way of performance management processes.

▨ An organisation does not have an appraisal process but many components of performance management are in place: coaching, objective setting, good performance information, etc.

▨ Some, or all, of the workforce have had experience of an appraisal process in the past with different employers. Those experiences may have been largely positive, largely negative or a mixture of both.

Each scenario poses the appraisal process designer with different challenges.

The organisation's history with appraisal and the employees' previous experience of appraisal form an important backdrop to appraisal design and introduction. Most managers or other employees will have an opinion about performance appraisal. Getting in touch with their experiences, good or bad, is an important part of designers' preparation.

current performance management

It is difficult to conceive of an organisation surviving for very long without a performance management process, even one that is not elaborate or even conscious. Figure 4.1 suggests that one issue at the centre of thinking about appraisal is an awareness of which aspects of a performance management process are currently in place. To introduce performance appraisal without establishing this risks wasting energy by duplicating procedures, or, perhaps worse, introducing performance appraisal unconnected with other practices in the organisation. It is wise to ask what will need to be changed or modified in the move towards a more conscious, deliberate performance management process.

The following areas should be considered when assessing the extent to which important elements of performance management are in place.

clarity of purpose and direction

Here we look at some important questions in order to develop a picture of the extent to which an organisation is clear about its purpose and direction.

how clear is the organisation about its purpose and direction?

The notion that an organisation is always crystal clear about its purpose, direction and the strategies it will pursue is largely unrealistic. Organisations are simply not like that. Achieving clarity can be difficult. There may be substantial uncertainties as the context within which organisations operate changes. Even at a senior level, people may interpret this in different ways, but even in these difficult circumstances it may be possible to have *sufficient* clarity to operate and to achieve excellence. Where there are uncertainties, it is usually possible to identify them. Better this than to throw one's hands in the air and say that things are so uncertain that is not possible to articulate vision, mission and short-term goals.

Coming back to the central point, there is little purpose in introducing appraisal when there is insufficient clarity as to what is to be appraised. A lack of clarity is most significant if it exists at senior level. If appraisal is to contribute to an organisation, those at senior levels will need to cascade objectives or take an informed view on the competencies that the appraisal process will address. If they can do neither then the appraisal process will rapidly behave like a lungfish. Where there is clarity of purpose and direction, the task for those designing and introducing an appraisal process is to make sure it helps the organisation fulfil that purpose.

communicating the big picture

It is one thing for senior managers to know the organisation's purpose and direction, but it is another to communicate it to employees in language that makes sense to them. The ability to sum up an organisation's purpose is a powerful leadership device, and one that provides a focus for the purpose of appraisal.

The President of the Parker Pen company's saying 'We are in the gift business' could be apocryphal, but it captures the idea of a manager/leader who has vision which, when articulated, provides a conceptual framework around which the company's people can muster. As we saw in Chapter 1, describing an adoption agency as being in the business of finding parents for children rather than children for parents could give a strong steer on what the organisation is trying to achieve.

In his introduction to an announcement of impending change, a director of a European heating fuel distribution company attempted to explain the nature of the business to a group of drivers and office staff in this way:

> Our business involves us having, across the country, a few very large holes in the ground full of fuel. Our job is to get the fuel into smaller holes in the ground or smallish size tanks slightly above the ground.

> What we need to do, is to do that at the lowest possible cost to our company, and at a price our customers are prepared to pay, and at a level of service our customers have the right to expect. Anything that stops us doing this has to change.

The staff he was talking to found this concise explanation very helpful. Simple, but not simplistic. The quotation won't win prizes and it is unlikely to feature in other books. It isn't slick, or even punchy by some standards, but it worked in that organisation.

Not all managers can make these connections, although they can learn to. Organisations need to spot the person most able to paint the big picture convincingly for the organisation as a whole. Ideally this should be the organisation's chief executive, president, etc. However, all managers at all levels need to reinforce the central message of what the business is and what its goals are. They also need to add a local flavour to the picture. An inspirational statement from the top does nothing to communicate purpose and direction unless the message is regularly repeated, in appropriate ways, in all parts of the organisation.

Those designing appraisal processes need to reflect upon the extent to which the organisation's purpose and direction is communicated. Their task is made easier when purpose and direction is communicated well, and much more difficult when it is not.

do staff realise the contribution they make or can make?

Adding a local flavour to the big picture helps only when the individual can see the picture and relate it to his or her job. Clarifying the role rather than the job or task list is also challenging, but from the example below we can see that it can be done.

During a consultancy assignment in a college I met a group of cleaners. I invited them to talk about the college and the nature of their work in order to establish how well the college was implementing its people management policies.

One of the cleaners spoke about her work as being about making the college look good for *adults*. She talked about the cleaners' contribution to the college's marketing effort, explaining that for the college to do well it needed a steady, increasing, flow of students. The college's main purpose was to deliver education and to provide learning opportunities for 16–18 year-olds but was subject to stiff competition.

Over several months their manager had explained to the cleaners that many young people came to the college only after their parents approved the choice. He had explained that parents were influenced by many things, including how the college looked and how safe it felt; having corridors and classrooms spotless and tidy was therefore very important.

Also, when cleaners were working towards the end of the afternoon some parents would collect their youngsters. In addition, adults enrolled for part-time and evening classes used the college while cleaning was still in progress. The cleaners recognised that they needed to operate safely and took pride in ensuring that cables and leads from their cleaning equipment did not constitute a hazard to any students.

The cleaners also explained that they were part of a 'graffiti alert'. Whenever they saw graffiti in or near the college their manager had made it clear they should immediately tell him, bringing him out of meetings if necessary. He had arranged with a local contractor that graffiti within the college's boundaries would be removed within one hour of his phone call. Their manager also did all that he could to ensure the rapid removal of graffiti in the college's environs.

The cleaners were as committed a group of employees as any I have met working in the UK education system.

Since this experience I have had little patience for managers who say that their people just do a job and cannot be expected to identify with the organisation's purposes and direction. This example underlines a key point: performance management is a day-to-day affair and not an episodic activity. It is the day-to-day reinforcement and feedback that gives it life. When designing an appraisal process it is important to work from where the organisation is, not from where we would like it to be. Tuning in to existing practice is very important.

expressing expectations and measuring performance

Appraisal processes often founder even where direction is clear and people are aware of the contribution they are asked to make. The leap from these broad concepts to what it means in practice for individuals' performance is too great. Sometimes no one knows what is to be measured. The following are areas to look at.

job descriptions
Up-to-date job descriptions help describe the job's required responsibilities, tasks and inputs, and also define its minimum requirements.

competencies
The organisation may identify behaviours, attitudes, knowledge and skills that people need to exhibit and develop in order to deliver acceptable or superior job performance, and pursue their objectives over the appraisal period of (say) a year.

The extent to which people know which competencies they need to bring to their job, and which they are expected to acquire, are important signs of their understanding of what is to be measured. If there is no habit of articulating the required competencies, the development of an appraisal process may stimulate an organisation to introduce competency frameworks before launching a fully-fledged appraisal process.

role descriptions

These help clarify the wider perspective of the role the post-holder is expected to play within the organisation. Knowing the part they play in an organisation helps people to place competencies in context.

Management by Objectives

To make role descriptions clearer, organisations tend to set objectives and targets, especially for managers, to indicate what the job-holder should deliver, typically through using Management by Objectives. They also identify changes in performance that are being looked for over the forthcoming period through setting improvement targets. Management by Objectives generally identifies the areas of the job's activities or 'key result areas' upon which the job-holder is expected to have an impact.

In organisations with conventional hierarchies both key result areas and objectives are translated and cascaded to those who report to the manager. For example, a works manager's key result areas could include production quantity, production quality, on-time delivery, production cost, stock control, machine and space utilisation, and health and safety. Those of the HR manager, reporting to the works manager, could include recruiting and selecting, training and consultancy, union–management relations, advice on people management issues accepted by managers, and advice leading to production improvements.

Each key result area can then be brought to life by spelling out the objectives. Objectives usually indicate the intention, direction and desired result. So, under the 'production cost' item the works manager may be expected to 'save money by reducing the proportion of rejected product by 5 per cent in the next 12 months'. To assist the works manager, the HR manager may have an objective 'to assist scrap reduction, increasing operator accuracy through identifying selection tests that provide reliable predictors of operator accuracy'.

SMART objectives

Most texts say that objectives should be SMART (Specific, Measurable, Achievable, Realistic and Time-bounded). However, my experience suggests that most objectives, and especially softer objectives that are difficult to measure, need an additional dimension. Spelling out the observable *behaviour* that should result from the objective being achieved can do this. Then judgements can be made on the extent to which the objective has been achieved by addressing the extent to which the behaviour is apparent.

For example, as a result of critical customer feedback a store manager might have an objective of:

> Over the next six months to find ways of working with and/or training staff so that established customers, through surveys, report that they feel more welcome in the store. If successful, customers will report that employees make eye contact and smile in a manner acceptable to customers.

Those designing and introducing performance appraisal need to know the extent to which objectives or other ways of expressing expectations and measuring performance are in place. Without some measures already in place or measures that can be introduced easily, appraisal is unlikely to deliver much to appraiser, appraisee or the organisation.

codes of conduct

Imagine what would happen to an appraisal process if at each appraisal a headteacher had to define and negotiate behaviour required of the school's teachers, or a manager in charge of engineering had to do the same with engineers. This uncomfortable situation can and does come about when aspects of performance management are under-developed.

Appraisal has a part to play in refining formal or informal codes of practice and how they relate to an individual, but it cannot be expected to generate codes of conduct. There is a strong case for formulating the codes well in advance of the introduction of appraisal. If the codes are explained at a job selection interview, it also clarifies for applicants what is expected of them. Not everyone takes to instructions that they have to smile at customers at least three times during each transaction at the supermarket checkout, so it is best for an applicant to know what is expected before taking the job.

It is helpful for those involved in introducing performance appraisal to ascertain whether codes of conduct are clear. If this can happen outside the appraisal process, it relieves appraisal of an unnecessary burden.

day-to-day behaviour

It is fairly common for official rules, whether written down or not, to conflict with the rules people follow day-by-day. It is also fairly common for appraisal to focus on the official rules even though they conflict with accepted practice.

Whether or not one agrees with the day-to-day practice it is vital for those designing the appraisal process to know in which version of reality the appraisal process is to be located. If the gap between espoused codes of practice and operating codes of practice is wide then the gap will need to be closed to a point where the appraisal process is dealing with the real organisation rather than some false picture.

training and development

The Hambleden Group identified 'hyper-growth' companies which trained their people and did so with a focus on business performance. This considered, pragmatic, approach to investing in the learning of the organisation is a major support to employee performance.

An organisation may or may not have the good habits of linking training and development to a job's requirements, and in turn to the organisation's goals. Without those habits it is difficult to run that part of an appraisal which asks the parties involved to identify training and development needs. Managers need to think through and support training and development that supports the organisation and helps the individual to do his or her job.

It is fairly common for managers to think of training and development solely in terms of off-job 'courses'. Indeed many managers seem unwilling or unable to identify what it is that those reporting to them need to learn. Instead they search for a course someone can go on. Because they do not try to understand the competence someone needs to develop, they do not search for different ways of helping others to acquire it, or for ways to extend the competence level at which someone is currently operating. There are many options other than course-based learning. Good managers consider the full repertoire given below.

Learning methods	
Mentoring – internal and external	Computer-based training
Coaching – internal and external	Carrying out research
Involvement in/carrying out projects	Learning 'networks'
'Sitting with Nellie' – shadowing/observing	Video/audio tapes
Taking on delegated tasks	Courses/workshops
Reading	Special assignments
Distance learning	Work exchanges
Open learning	Planned experience

Another inhibitor to the successful introduction and implementation of appraisal is managers' erroneous assumptions as to who is responsible for training. Many managers in medium-sized organisations with underdeveloped performance management processes assume that training is the responsibility of the training department, not their own responsibility.

Managers' attitudes and assumptions regarding their responsibility for training need to be assessed before the introduction of performance appraisal. Introducing appraisal in itself is unlikely to be sufficient to shift attitudes and assumptions about the nature of and responsibility for training.

Designers of appraisal processes will need to clarify the responsibilities of the parties involved in appraisal for defining the appraisee's learning goals and how the learning goals are to be met.

managers as coaches

Most people need some help to learn how to do their job better or differently or to learn a new aspect of their job. One of the most powerful ways of helping people learn is through coaching, placing emphasis on helping people to learn rather than on teaching or training.

The critical issue is the establishment of a relationship between the manager-coach and the employee-learner where the learner is willing and able to learn from the coach. Good coaching involves helping the learner to remove internal blocks to learning as much as providing hints and tips, advice and information.

Some managers are natural coaches, others struggle, and others do not even think of operating as a coach. Appraisal provides good coaches with a steer on what coaching needs to take place. The more the individual believes that good, sensitive coaching will follow on from appraisal, the more energy they will put into the appraisal process.

The more high-quality coaching that goes on in an organisation the more chance there is of appraisal making a contribution. If there is little or no evidence of coaching then this needs to be taken into account by those designing and introducing appraisal.

career development

Organisations vary in the degree to which they are inclined to support learning where the pay-off is long term and difficult to forecast. Some will support employee training and development even when there is little evidence that it will benefit the organisation. While some reserve development for those who are seen to be the future stars of the organisation, others spread development effort and expenditure thinly. In yet another category are those organisations that do not spend on learning activities unless there is a readily identifiable short-term pay-off.

My experience is that not to have a policy on support for career development activities or not to declare it is the worst state of affairs. This leaves appraisers and appraisees unclear about whether it is acceptable to raise the topic of training and development for career purposes at the appraisal discussion. It can lead to arguments in the discussion as to the legitimacy or otherwise of introducing the topic. In some organisations the ambiguity distorts and discredits the appraisal process.

It may be surprising, but some organisations have a policy of not supporting career development activities, but still include a consideration of career potential and development matters in their appraisal. A good deal of time and energy is saved if people know that the organisation will do little or nothing to support people's career aspirations. They may not like the policy, but at least know where they stand and do not spend time speculating or trying to discover what the policy is.

Organisations that are committed to supporting career development need their managers to actively support the policy and also to have the skills to act as career counsellors. Managers also need the insight to know when it is best to refer the individual to someone else in the organisation, for example their own manager, and know what resources, if any, are available to fund careers guidance support outside the organisation.

skills needed to handle appraisals

Most appraisal processes of merit require a wide range of thinking and interpersonal skills to cover the appraisal agenda. Appraisers need a reasonable level of data-gathering and analytical skills, and skills of eliciting and presenting thoughts, ideas and information. An appraisal discussion can generate emotions in appraiser and appraisee, and the appraiser also needs to be able to handle both sets of emotions. Critical to the success of most appraisal discussions is the ability to negotiate and agree follow-through action to which both parties are committed. The skills required are not relevant only for appraisal, of course: the managers use them to manage their people day-to-day.

Unless there is a reasonable level of interpersonal and analytical skill present in the organisation, the demands of an appraisal process will be too great. If the skills are lacking, the situation may be saved through an investment in interpersonal skills training in addition to good training for appraisers and appraisees. Alternatively the appraisal process may be designed to suit the skill level of those involved. It would be reckless to proceed to implementing an appraisal scheme without assessing and addressing the prevalent interpersonal skills of appraisers and appraisees.

remuneration

Remuneration practices convey messages as to what gets rewarded and also what does not.

Tom Lupton and Dan Gowler published a very significant book in the 1960s which remains a definitive book on how to construct wage payment systems for 'shop floor' personnel. They suggest that payment systems reward *time* placed at the employer's disposal, *energy* expended to generate output or worker *competence and/or performance*, and combinations of these different types of 'effort'. In addition, a conscious or less conscious decision is taken as to the major unit of accountability. The units to be rewarded can be the individual worker, the work-team or the organisation as a whole. An organisation is likely to feel different to work in according to what is rewarded. For example, where an individual's earnings are based on the quality and/or quantity of product produced by the team of which he or she is a part, the organisation will feel different to one where earnings are contingent on skills demonstrated by the individual.

Other aspects of performance management may reinforce or moderate the messages conveyed by the payment system. Payment systems are crude instruments and need fine-tuning at times. The crude message that, say, what matters is the competence of individuals, may need to be supported or moderated from elsewhere in the performance management package. It may be important to stress that the quantity and quality of output is also valued, even though it may be difficult to measure accurately enough to include in the payment system's rules.

There is an understandable temptation to use appraisal processes to do the fine-tuning and to attempt to reinforce or moderate the pay system's messages. Those responsible for designing and implementing appraisal processes need to know the extent to which pay is to be linked with performance appraisal. To link or not to link appraisal judgements with pay is probably the most controversial issue in the design of a performance appraisal process. The key arguments in the debate are set out below.

The case for a link with pay:

▨ When individuals demonstrate that their performance is at or above that expected, or do well against demanding objectives, they should receive financial recognition above and beyond base salary.

▨ As pressure for organisation performance increases, people who help to deliver that performance or make a bigger contribution than other employees doing similar jobs should be rewarded.

▨ 'Equal pay for unequal performance is in no one's interest: it doesn't reward excellence or encourage improvements' – Prime Minister Tony Blair, June 1999.

▨ High performers will leave employers and join organisations where performance is rewarded.

▨ When there is a clear link between effort and performance it should be rewarded.

▨ In any work-team its members will know its top performers; to claim otherwise is naïve.

The case against a link with pay:

▨ It is difficult to assess performance in complex jobs fairly; the link between individual performance and behaviour, results and pay is very difficult to demonstrate; it is easier to offend than satisfy people.

▨ Differentiating between people works against team effort.

▨ Pay links wreck the authenticity of appraisal discussion because it discourages helpful candour.

▨ Performance-related pay gets in the way of improvement (see Deming's criticisms later in this chapter).

▨ For pay to be an incentive it is necessary to pay some 10–15 per cent above base salary: unaffordable when times are hard and only attainable in the public sector by paying average performers considerably below what they could earn in the private sector.

The debate is important and problematic. For a more detailed discussion see Frank Hartle's book, Chapter 9.

For our purposes the key point is that a robust performance management process is likely to take up a position on the link between pay and performance. After all, while it is possible to have performance management and appraisal without a pay link, it is unlikely that an organisation can implement a worthwhile performance pay policy without other aspects of performance management, including appraisal.

If an organisation's position on performance pay and the link between it and appraisal is ambiguous then appraisal process designers need to have the position clarified. To introduce performance appraisal without knowing how much the appraisal process will inform pay decisions is asking for trouble.

appraisal as part of performance management

As we have already seen, performance appraisal needs to be part of an authentic performance management process if it is to contribute to the organisation's success.

The trick is to have all the elements in the process mutually supportive, relevant to the organisation and actively implemented by managers at all levels. Unless the performance management process becomes a key foundation of running the organisation, it will at best underdeliver, and appraisal with it. At worst, it will take the organisation backwards: it takes up time that could have been better used, raises expectations that are not met and reduces the chance of appraisal being successfully reintroduced in the future.

people management
the day-to-day

Managing people is not just about implementing formal performance management processes. The manager's perceived interest in supporting high performance, and the relationships between managers and their people, are shaped by what happens between them every day. They are also shaped by what does not happen between them. For example, a manager's enthusiasm or indifference when telling a member of staff that a customer has expressed delight with his or her service conveys a message. The sense of excitement, or of weary resignation, from the boss when announcing an addition to the product range also sends a signal to employees. People learning about the introduction of a new product or service in the press before the manager gets round to telling them also leaves its mark.

Contrast these cameos with the manager's delight at hearing of satisfied customers, at announcing a new strand to the department's service, and when thanking a member of staff for supporting colleagues in another part of the organisation. Small incidents contribute to the overall message about how people and their performance are valued.

Important though the day-to-day is, there are other people management practices that need to be taken into account in order to prepare for designing and introducing or reintroducing appraisal. These are outlined below.

succession management

The environments within which most organisations operate have become more uncertain and unstable over the last few decades. We have witnessed the demise of the attempt by organisations to forecast the need for and manage the provision of the number and type of employees: manpower planning, as it was known in the 1970s. Support for equal opportunities policies has called into question the ethics of grooming favoured people for promotion and has led to more open approaches to filling jobs.

We have already noted that the extent to which an organisation is prepared to support career development is a factor in the context in which appraisal is designed, introduced and run. An organisation is more likely to support career development if there is some open attempt to manage succession.

There are instances when those designing the appraisal process are pressed to include 'potential assessment' within the performance appraisal process. They would be wise to resist such pressure because it overburdens the appraisal process and in particular the appraisal discussion. In larger organisations, other than those operating what Charles Handy (1978) describes as a 'club' culture, identifying potential successors is usually better addressed through a separate process. This can be managed through openly inviting applicants for 'fast-track' systems or encouraging people to discuss their aspirations. This can provide a pool of talented people whose particular career aspirations are known, and can be harnessed to serve the organisation.

However, it is also common to find that assessments of people's potential to make career moves do not correlate with assessments of performance in appraisal. In other words it is possible for there to be an inexplicable mismatch between appraisal ratings and assessment for potential ratings. Such a paradox does harm to both appraisal and to succession planning. This apparent contradiction is something those designing, introducing and implementing appraisal need to avoid.

use of competencies

The identification and use of competencies indicates to employees what behaviour and performance the organisation values. An organisation using competencies for recruitment and selection, for assessing promotability, for identifying training and development needs and, of course, for appraisal, signals that it takes this tool very seriously indeed. It is quite possible to manage performance and introduce an appraisal process without formally adopting a competency-based approach: many organisations do. Not using competencies, however, reduces the power of performance management processes and appraisal.

Organisations may be attracted to the notion of competencies because competencies are concerned with the application of skills and knowledge to generate *acceptable performance* rather than just the raw skill or knowledge. There is also an attraction in being able to spot a cluster of competencies that leads to acceptable job performance.

At the risk of offending practitioners I would argue that the notion of 'acceptable' as opposed to 'exceptional' performance is a UK perspective strongly embedded in the National Vocational Qualifications (NVQ) movement.

An alternative approach is based on ideas developed mostly in the USA, represented by, for example, Hay/McBer's approach to competencies. Here, competencies are manifestations of an individual's inner drives, traits, self-concepts, skills and knowledge. Most importantly, the identification of these competencies predicts not acceptable performance, but *exceptional* job performance, based on extensive research.

There is increasing interest in the application of the notion of emotional intelligence and in the Emotional Competence Inventory. Developed for Hay/McBer by Daniel Goleman, who popularised emotional intelligence, Richard Boyatzis, a leading competency practitioner, and others at Hay, the Emotional Competence Inventory identifies the emotional competencies and the level of operation of the competencies that lead to highly effective performance.

To many of my clients the attraction of the NVQ approach is the availability of ready-made competency frameworks that build a picture of acceptable performance devised for specific occupations or specific sectors. Adopting such an approach allows hard-pressed HR managers to lift administrative, management or customer care competencies, among others, 'off the shelf'. NVQs also provide a set of more narrowly focused competencies, eg for technicians operating in electronic engineering companies.

Organisations more interested in identifying competencies for exceptional performance may be prepared to fund studies to identify the competency frameworks. For example, two such studies funded by the UK government have identified the competencies of highly effective headteachers and teachers.

There is also interest in identifying those competencies that will generate success in particular organisations. Such tailor-made competencies may be more attractive to larger organisations. To be able to identify what makes the best stand out from the rest, there needs to be a sufficient number of exceptional performers in a particular occupational group to use as a benchmark.

It is important to recognise that placing value on competencies that generate *acceptable* performance sends a different message from placing value on competencies that, if demonstrated, yield *exceptional* performance.

Not using competencies at all increases the burden on managers to work out and explain what behaviours are required. In addition, failure to recognise the value of competencies may send out the message that there is little interest in *how* people do what they do and how their competency improves. The focus is on what the person achieves rather than how he or she achieves it. This way of thinking may be perfectly valid, of course, but it does influence the way in which people are managed.

In short, if organisations opt for including competencies as part of their people management practices, they need to consider whether these will be used to define acceptable or exceptional performance, and whether they will use a set of 'off-the-shelf' or 'custom built' competencies. These choices will all shape the context in which appraisal operates.

teamwork

As we saw when we looked at the impact of culture, some individuals work as part of a team, with each team-member's performance impacting on that of the others. The process work culture values and recognises teamwork skills. However, in functional work cultures the individual's performance is critical. (See Figure 4.2). While individuals may need to work collaboratively with others and avoid destructive conflict, it is the behaviour and output of the individual that it is important to influence and recognise.

Taking extreme views, we can therefore predict that where team cohesion, performance and output is what counts, just using individual appraisal may be counterproductive. The mixed message 'the team is all but we'll only appraise individuals' is as difficult to live with as the message 'the individual's performance is what matters but we'll only appraise the team'.

In many instances there is a middle ground. Both individual and team performance matter. Appraisal processes need to be designed to reflect the extent to which individuals are expected to contribute to team performance. Chapter 8 examines team appraisal.

management style

Some years back a fellow consultant once worked with a leading supermarket chain. He described their managers as adhering to the 'Look here, Sunshine' school of management. In his view, most managers had a confrontational approach to managing people, and were on the alert for conflict and insubordination. The company had a 'hire-fire' reputation. He knew that the predominant management style was not company policy but it was a well-established norm of managerial behaviour. Yet in other organisations, either by design or through custom and practice, the reverse can be true. Managers are highly consultative and adopt participative and inclusive ways of working, even to the extent of avoiding the confrontation of marginal or mediocre performance.

In a third type of organisation, it is difficult to detect a dominant style or establish what the commended style is because managerial style varies with the personal preferences of each manager or as a considered response to the current context of their areas of responsibility.

An appraisal process tends to be moulded to suit the organisation's predominant management style. Hard-edged processes where there are implications for job retention and pay call for directive, confrontational, no-nonsense styles. Other processes call upon managers to act as patient facilitators, good listeners and cast the manager in the role of friend and helper.

An appraisal process can be in or out of tune with the prevailing management style. Those developing the process need to identify the approved or dominant style, and be aware of the extent to which the appraisal process will mirror or challenge the existing style.

evaluation and improvement of people management

The tendency to be reflective and flexible when it comes to evaluating people management practices, or just to 'get on with it', varies from organisation to organisation. It is tempting to dive into improvements without having done the work to understand why the current approach is not working. Even when practices are evaluated and improved, the efficiency and effectiveness with which improvement is achieved may also vary.

I know an organisation where two sets of reviews and improvements to people management practices took place at the same time without those involved in the reviews knowing that both developments were taking place. In another organisation a group charged with developing an appraisal process for sales people was working in isolation from another group charged with investigating and changing the commission system for sales people. The appraisal process was destined to support collaboration between sales people and cross-functional collaboration, while the commission system was intended to stimulate and reward the performance of individuals. These two tracks could be made to work together but only did so when the two groups responsible for the rethinking worked collaboratively.

Appraisal designers need to know what changes and improvements to people management practices are under way or planned. They can then decide whether they want to influence other changes or reflect other changes and improvements in their work on appraisal.

relationship between appraiser and appraisee

Appraisal works best when the appraiser and appraisee normally have a productive relationship. It seems to me that two critical conditions need to be met: the appraisee must have well-developed self-awareness; and the appraisee must respect the appraiser's skills in feeding back information, judgements, and informed opinion.

Appraisees who have insight into their own performance and their own strengths and weaknesses usually welcome the opportunity to test out their perceptions.

Where there is an established appraisal process the appraisee will already have a view on the extent to which he or she is prepared to pay attention to the appraiser's feedback and

opinions. In organisations where there is no formal performance appraisal process the appraisee will have a conscious or
less conscious view of the extent to which he or she will respect
the appraiser's skills and judgements. This will impact upon the
outcome of appraisal discussions when a process is introduced.
A guide to the consequences of the position on the two axes
appears in Figure 4.4.

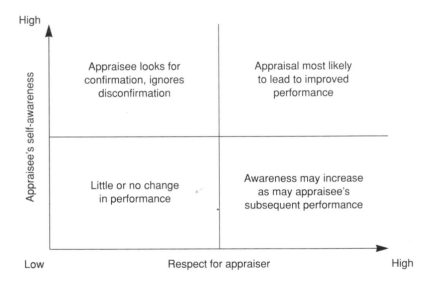

Figure 4.4   *Appraisee's self-awareness/respect for appraiser*

When the appraisee has well-developed self-awareness and
respects the appraiser, the appraisal discussion is likely to lead
to an accurate assessment of appraisee performance. Such a
discussion usually results in a workable action plan on what
needs to be done to maintain or increase the appraisee's performance. The other quadrants in Figure 4.4 suggest other less
optimistic forecasts of outcome.

Those with the remit to design and implement a performance appraisal process should make an estimate of the current pattern of relationships. If there is evidence of productive working relationships between appraisers and appraisees, designers need to predict whether introducing appraisal or modifications to an existing process will support rather than disrupt those relationships. They must also predict whether the appraisal process will help turn problematic relationships into productive ones, or exacerbate existing difficulties in working relationships. These predictions can steer the designers' actions.

If the designers conclude that few of the relationships are likely to yield positive outcomes from appraisal they may decide to test this view and investigate its cause, eg through a survey or other form of investigation. Identifying the cause of the relationship problems is critical. These may, for example, be due to lack of confidence in the managers' ability to base their judgements on evidence as opposed to prejudice or essentially personal opinions. It may be necessary to train managers so that they command more respect and the confidence of their people.

fundamental human considerations
power imbalance

In an article on research into the nature and impact of appraisal, Tim Newton and Patricia Findlay point to the unequal relationship between a manager acting as appraiser, and an employee. Appraisal can be viewed as one instrument in the manager's portfolio of control methods. At some level people know this. Some, but not all, resent it.

Those in 'professional' organisations – engineers, scientists, teachers, social workers and so on – may be particularly conscious of the inequality between manager-as-appraiser and appraisee. Where norms of managers being the first among equals and of individualism exist, there are often overt and covert attempts to challenge the need for appraisal. If the need is accepted, there are ways in which it can be implemented that do not conflict with the organisation's collegiate culture: for example, a process of assisted self-review with the appraisee choosing who will act as appraiser (as shown in Figure 5.2 in the next chapter); or peer appraisal where colleagues review each other's performance.

Organisations that have peer appraisal processes report mixed results. The main difficulty is with the follow-through after the appraisal discussion: often little action results. Unless appraisees are able to agree on actions that the appraisee implements through self-development, peer appraisal processes tend to disappoint. Normally, peers do not have the power to implement decisions reached in the appraisal discussion. Appraisees still need to access resources, for example for training and development. Peer appraisal therefore just defers the point at which appraisees are reminded that someone else has more control than they do.

Much of the history of appraisal is concerned with reducing or putting aside issues of power imbalance. Some would have us believe that a manager can happily operate both as judge and counsellor, even when appraisal is pay-related. I know that there are managers who can conduct the appraisal process and the appraisal discussion in ways that dampen the negative effect of the judge–helper tensions. However, doings so requires high levels of interpersonal skills and such practice is not that common.

Not all managers can operate appraisal in a way that makes all employees comfortable with all that takes place during an appraisal. Can we really see the day when everyone is open about his or her weaknesses, readily contemplates demotion or is relaxed about not getting a performance payment because his or her appraisal rating does not merit it?

The power imbalance does have its positive side. I am not suggesting for one moment that it should not exist. My concern is that it should be recognised and not denied or ignored. The position-power of managers and leaders is critical for the purposes of keeping people on board and on track, and appraisal helps to achieve those things. Appraisal helps *management* to address staffing issues and to control people, and to anticipate and solve problems. It also contributes to *leadership* by helping to align people and motivate and inspire them.

There are many reasons why appraisers and appraisees may be uncomfortable with appraisal. These reasons will be expressed in several ways, some of which come down to the power imbalance and some that are triggered by other concerns. Whatever the concerns, they will need to be heard and acknowledged if appraisal is to take place in the right climate.

managers' dislike of conducting appraisals

Here is a sample from a range of objections frequently voiced by managers:

- having to complete a substantial number of appraisal assessments and discussions in a narrow 'window' – 'I rattle through them because I've got eight to do in two weeks';
- an uncomfortable feeling about judging people or others knowing that this is happening – 'I didn't like judging people behind closed doors and now it's all in the open and people get to see the forms I feel even worse about it';
- lack of confidence that agreement made with the appraisee will be followed through – 'There's little

point in agreeing things if the company doesn't deliver.
I don't like letting people down';

■ not wanting to tackle performance deficiencies – 'I
think we should keep things positive. I don't think
there is much I can achieve by forcing someone to look
at his or her weaknesses. I don't want to upset people I
then have to work with for the rest of the year';

■ a feeling that formal appraisals are unnecessary – 'I'm
always appraising those who report to me';

■ appraisal processes which are too demanding – 'I have
to look back at performance over the last year, spell
out what the department is expected to do over the
next year, agree new performance targets, review
behaviour against a string of competencies, define
training and development needs, have a career discussion if the person wants it, talk about how I can be of
more help. I do all this without having had an
appraisal from my boss first!';

■ the time it takes is not worthwhile – 'I don't get as
much out of it as I put into it';

■ appraisal is a pointless paperchase – 'There's an eight-
page form. I have to sign it, the appraisee has to sign it.
My boss has to sign it. HR want a copy of the last two
pages, and what for?';

■ the process asks managers to do unnecessary things,
such as observe the appraisee at work – 'We meet, e-
mail each other and talk on the phone but I rarely see
my people selling. I can meet my sales target for the
region without seeing them operate. I'm not going to
shadow them just to fill in an appraisal form.'.

Objections can be heartfelt reasons or convenient excuses.
What is clear is that they cannot be ignored. It would be foolish
to devise an appraisal processes without acknowledging some
of the disquiet expressed by appraisers who are being asked to
conduct a revised process or those who will be appraising

under a process being introduced for the first time. It helps if the introduction is phased, and that there is a commitment to evaluate and revise the process in the light of the evaluation.

Appraisal designers will be heartened to know that some managers enjoy appraisal. They put a lot into it and get a lot out of it. Managers who have good things to say about appraisal need to be identified and encouraged to act as role models and champions for the process within the organisation.

appraisees' dislike of appraisals

Although some appraisees derive considerable benefit from appraisal many do not, or anticipate that they will not. Some of the main criticisms I have encountered are from:

- Appraisees who feel intruded upon. They just like getting on with their work and see little purpose in an appraisal discussion.
- Employees who are more or less doing the same job now as they did a year ago. They may not accept that they have anything to learn and do not see the need for improvement. Some will feel the need to invent training needs and improvement areas just to have something to say, while feeling unhappy about doing so.
- Appraisees who do not like the thought of entering appraisal discussions where they fear they will be criticised. They are not sure how they will react if they feel under attack and can be concerned about being persuaded to agree to unachievable targets.
- People who are reluctant to look at their strengths: they can feel embarrassed. They may also be concerned about being under pressure to develop competence in areas where they feel they can never learn.

Some people fear that performance criteria are only partly declared. Sometimes these fears are justified. Again, to ignore appraisees' concerns would be unwise. Good managers can do a great deal to eliminate or reduce the impact of these concerns; less effective managers find this difficult. Many people want to be appraised and look forward to a constructive dialogue with their manager at appraisal time.

There is a strong case for identifying and handling the justifiable or unnecessary fears appraisees have in advance of the launch or relaunch of an appraisal process, especially in the Exacting HR culture referred to earlier.

understanding the issues

Some of the concerns outlined above will be easier to address if those responsible for implementing performance appraisal have considered the following questions:

what's in it for me?

It becomes easier to answer this question once one knows what the concerns and fears are and when the organisation, especially the senior management, knows why they want an appraisal process.

It is probably not possible to convince everyone that appraisal has genuine benefits to offer them. All organisations have their resident cynics. The important thing is that managers show a genuine interest in attempting to answer the question. Slick internal PR will not do. Organisations that proceed on the assumption that the benefits are obvious can end up with serious employee relations difficulties.

In the next chapter we will look in some detail at possible reasons and payoffs for having an appraisal process.

judgements against undisclosed criteria

I once did some work in an organisation where, in passing, a senior manager spoke about his concern about Michael, a recently appointed graduate. A young man of exceptional ability, he was making a contribution far in excess of what was expected of someone of his age and limited experience.

The senior manager was concerned about Michael's dress sense. Michael wore crumpled suits, poorly ironed shirts and his tie was seldom neatly knotted in place. The manager believed that the way Michael dressed could limit his social acceptability and his longer-term promotion prospects.

I asked if the manager had spoken to Michael about this. The manager replied with surprise. 'Oh no! We expect people to be sensitive enough to pick up the fact that almost everyone dresses in a particular and acceptable way. Anyway I imagine someone has dropped some subtle hints by now.'

So spotting the hidden code was one of the undisclosed criteria of success. Not recognising the code would probably blight Michael's career, and probably without him knowing.

It is the existence, or the fear of the existence, of undeclared rules, which puts some people off appraisal. Also, despite any assurances that appraisal does not lead to decisions about career moves and promotion, people may believe that it does. This is especially the case when there is no separate and transparent process for voicing career aspirations and for receiving feedback on how an individual's potential is regarded.

hunger for feedback

An organisation needs its appraisers to recognise the part appraisal plays in reinforcing behaviour that generates results, in getting people to stop doing some things and improve at others.

Managers and others in an organisation need to experience and value good feedback for appraisal to deliver its benefits. Effective feedback takes place between adults who respect each other. The recipient wants it, and wants to be with someone who is making valid observations rather than being judgmental and critical. The most useful feedback enables the recipient to change the way he or she operates because it focuses on aspects they can do something about. We are, of course, looking at the creation of a virtuous circle. People will be hungrier for feedback if that provided is of high quality and is perceived to be fair and useful.

How can the conditions to stimulate a hunger for feedback be created? The usual argument is that this has to start from the top. This may be true but how can it be achieved? In my experience one should not seek feedback within the organisation in the first instance, but develop the habit of systematically seeking and receiving good-quality feedback from *outside* the organisation, in particular from customers. As we saw in Chapter 1, excellent organisations really want this, are prepared to act upon it, and demonstrate that they do. A culture that welcomes and acts on customer feedback is much more likely to establish a habit of individuals receiving and valuing feedback from their internal customers.

The task of appraisal designers is much easier if the organisation habitually seeks and welcomes feedback. When interest in and ability to receive this is low, the task of running an effective appraisal process will be very challenging indeed.

is feedback helpful or a personal assault?

Some argue that feedback is likely to be of value or to be acted on only if the person wants to receive it. No matter how skilfully feedback is given, it will be unwelcome for some.

This is not to argue that one should stay only with the positive. To hold people accountable sometimes means that accurate but less favourable comments need to be made on some occasions. It is entirely appropriate for an appraiser to express concerns during the appraisal especially if a 'less than satisfactory' performance rating is a fair assessment. A discussion of what needs to happen for performance to improve also needs to take place.

For appraisal to be effective, a constructive relationship between appraiser and appraisee needs to be maintained. Destructively expressed criticism has no place in an appraisal process. Introducing into the appraisal discussion serious criticism or concerns about performance that have not been previously mentioned is usually unwise. As we will explore more fully later, an appraisal discussion should hold no unpleasant surprises.

what do we do with the gurus' criticisms?

Dr W Edwards Deming, a major figure in the Total Quality Management movement, made many references to the dysfunctions of appraisal. He proposed that differences in performance can be explained by problems with the way in which work and decision-making processes are set up.

According to Deming, appraisal encourages people to work around systems and processes rather than change them. He was particularly critical of performance appraisal processes that link merit payments to performance ratings. For Deming, targets and objectives that focus on functional or territorial boundaries work against teamwork as do those that focus on the individual. He also criticised Management by Objectives for leading to the setting of either barely attainable, or unattainable targets, or 'safe' targets that do not challenge processes and which are therefore unhelpful to the customer.

Members of the British Deming Association suggest there are ways to handle the criticism in their publication 'Performance Appraisal and all that!'. They suggest that replacing performance-related pay and performance appraisal requires 'an overhaul of the processes of management'. Senior management, according to the authors, needs to have instituted substantial improvements in how the organisation operates before looking to appraisal and performance-related pay to assist further improvements. They also argue that the bundle of activities which make up appraisal needs to be disaggregated and examined separately. The activities listed are: merit pay, performance objectives, promotion, salary levels, career planning, assessing training and development needs and reviewing past performance.

In effect, the publication begins to assert one of the central themes of this book, that various aspects of what we can call 'performance management' can, properly connected, be of benefit to organisations. It is bundling them together, calling them appraisal and then not allowing each component to make its own distinct coordinated contribution which causes trouble. Therefore, what appears to be a challenge by one of the foremost critics of appraisal can be seen to be an attack on 'old-style' appraisal. The new-style appraisal discussed in this book is an appraisal set in a performance management context, one that is sensitive to the complexity of what influences performance and not one which peddles a false promise.

key questions

This chapter deals with the key questions that need to be answered to work towards introducing or modifying an appraisal process. The emphasis is on appraisal processes that will take an organisation forward.

the purpose of appraisal

The designers of a performance appraisal process need answers to key questions to shape its design, introduction, implementation and monitoring. One vital but often avoided question is: 'What is appraisal for?'. Some organisations find it strange that people ask this. The answer may seem obvious. Often it is not. If we ask instead how people use appraisal, we end up with a list that is not necessarily comfortable to read. Appraisal can be used for constructive and less than constructive purposes. I have known performance appraisal to be used to:

- introduce major change, including change in an organisation's culture;
- define goals, targets and objectives for the forthcoming period;

- give people targets which are impossible to attain, as a means of firing them later;
- give the *appearance* that the organisation is interested in challenging employees to deliver high performance;
- review past performance in order to evaluate it and associate pay rewards with it;
- lobby appraisers for political, and even dubious, ends;
- gain special favours;
- agree learning goals;
- identify and plan to build on strengths;
- identify and plan to eliminate weaknesses;
- establish a constructive dialogue about performance that can be continued after the appraisal discussion;
- build on the existing dialogue between managers and their people;
- keep the parent company or a major stakeholder happy but with no intention of using appraisal to run the organisation.

key question 1

what problems is performance appraisal trying to solve or what opportunities is it trying to grasp?

Without clear answers to this key question, appraisal designers will be trying to steer a rudderless ship. They need to start by listing the agreed purposes – the 'official' position. It is likely that the final list will be tested and amended as they work through the other issues in this chapter and those in the outer circle of Figure 4.1.

The process designer will need to accept the challenge of surfacing the extent to which managers, especially senior managers, are committed to appraisal.

Some managers will say, 'We need an appraisal system' in

very much the same way they will say, 'We need to paint the exterior of the building'. Sadly, the realisation that appraisal is about relationships between people, sensitivities, as well as performance, escapes some managers.

Although ideal, it may be unrealistic to anticipate unbridled enthusiasm from all managers. Some managers need help in understanding what they will have to commit themselves to, so that their commitment is authentic.

Designers can test commitment to appraisal by identifying three issues at an early stage. These are: what managers, especially senior managers, will need to do; the time it will take; what managers, again, especially senior managers, will need to do to make the process live. Designers will also need to work with managers to identify the benefits of doing the work. These discussions usually help to flush out the stance that managers are truly taking.

An indication of the lack of real commitment at senior levels is the suggestion, often made at the top, that they do not need an appraisal in any form. They may suggest that appraisal belongs at middle management level or lower. In these circumstances, designers may be able to discuss the difficulties they anticipate given the senior managers' stance. This can lead to a call for managers to adjust their position or to abandon the introduction of appraisal.

In some circumstances those charged with introducing or modifying the appraisal process may not be prepared to take the risk of challenging managers. The debate may be perceived as impertinent, even to introduce it may be considered risky and 'career limiting'. However, not to do so is just storing trouble for later for the person charged with introducing or re-introducing appraisal. For external consultants it may result in not being paid or losing a client.

key question 2

will managers do what is required to get the most out of the appraisal process given its purpose?

Sadly, in some organisations, those responsible for design or implementation of performance appraisal are told to carry on even if they are able to demonstrate insufficient commitment to the process. Some senior managers do not face realities. Difficulties can result from the organisation's managers not owning the agenda. That may be driven by a parent company, a regulatory body or a major customer looking for appraisal to be in place, for example, as evidence of an organisation's interest in improvement. My advice to designers in this unfortunate position is to indulge in damage limitation; to develop an appraisal process that they believe will do some good, or at worst do no harm even if it will not do much good. This is a realistic and responsible response in the circumstances. Designing a modest process which managers will support affords the opportunity to build on practice in the future and come up with a process that genuinely contributes to the organisation's success.

key question 3

is there the right degree of openness to suit the purpose?

Consider these two real-life examples, both in the electronics industry, drawn from my practice.

Company A

Once a year those on management grades are subject to an appraisal undertaken by a panel. The panel is made up of an individual's manager, his or her manager and a manager in the next grade up from the appraisee but from another department or function. A personnel officer chairs the panel meeting. The appraisee is *not* invited. The conclusions are recorded and occasionally, but not always, used as a basis for merit pay assessment and for deciding a training and development plan.

There is no requirement to involve the individual being appraised before or after the appraisal panel meeting. It is unclear whether involving the individual is against company policy or not. What is clear is that the document summarising the panel's discussion and findings, the performance rating and potential rating are not to be shown to the appraisee.

A minority of managers discuss the fact that the appraisal is about to take place. Some discuss the main topics upon which the individual would like to receive feedback and the individual's view of his or her future and training needs. Some discuss the appraisal panel's main findings, and some jointly agree a training and development plan with the appraisee in response to the appraisal findings.

Company B

Four weeks before an appraisal discussion is to take place the electronics engineer and appraiser meet for around 20 minutes to agree the main themes that they'll discuss at the appraisal meeting. Both agree the information that needs to be found to aid the discussion, much of which they have used to run progress/review meetings over the last 11 months.

Both know that the meeting will focus on performance, and that there is an indirect link between the appraisal meeting and the pay award to be made 3 months after appraisal discussions have been conducted with all team members. They also know the appraisee can meet the appraiser's boss for a career discussion should the appraisee want to.

In most cases the appraiser and appraisee have a good, adult, straightforward working relationship. There is little chance of either party being offended or surprised by the nature of the feedback they give to each other.

They will agree what is recorded on the appraisal document and both know the minimum record required. The appraiser's boss can read the record of the meeting and its main decisions. Otherwise the form remains confidential to the appraisee and appraiser.

It is fairly obvious that Company B's appraisal process has a much better chance of contributing to the organisation's success than that of Company A. Transparency, and even more importantly, the belief that the process is transparent, increases appraisees' commitment to appraisal. Company A's performance appraisal process is indeed 'closed door'. There is very little transparency and what there is exists because rumour alone spreads the knowledge that there is a process and that some managers operate it differently to others. Company B is much more open and trusting of the parties involved. There is real encouragement for dialogue without unnecessary pressure. Appraisees are more likely to have confidence in the process and to know that their views matter.

Although nowadays there would be a weak case for adopting an approach similar to Company A's, there is still a tendency for some organisations to be secretive about their appraisal methods. Even if they have good reason for secrecy organisations need to recognise the limitations of this and consider whether such an approach contributes to or detracts from the core purpose of appraisal.

In Chapter 3 we outlined tools to plot organisational culture. At this stage, designers would be well advised to use the tools to answer some important questions:

▨ What are the prevailing work and HR cultures in the organisation?
▨ Is the intention to design a performance appraisal process to fit, or to change, the prevailing culture?
▨ Are there design criteria that need to be agreed in advance in order to fit or change the culture?

key question 4

to what extent is the appraisal process likely to be in sympathy with, or expected to influence, the organisation's culture?

Again, checking back to the core purpose of appraisal, process designers need to know if the intention is to change aspects of an organisation's culture via the introduction or redesign of appraisal. If other initiatives are in hand to contribute to a change in culture, designers need to develop a good working relationship with those involved. If designers are expected to change an organisation's culture without cooperation from others involved, or indeed with appraisal as the only instrument, they face an awesome, and probably impossible, task.

Designers need to examine the current or likely connection/disconnection between appraisal and the rest of the performance management process (as described in detail in Chapter 4). As we already know, performance appraisal is just one tool in the performance management toolkit. It is important to determine the contribution that appraisal is expected to make to introducing or embedding performance management.

key question 5

are there sufficient links with the rest of the performance management process?

To answer this question, those designing the performance appraisal process may need to survey the organisation, formally or informally.

A performance management process may not be enshrined in obvious systems or schemes but nonetheless may be in place, at least in part. Some good day-to-day feedback may go on, many managers may be operating as effective coaches and some managers may have found inspiring ways of articulating the organisational mission.

Let's look at three possible answers to the question:

'*Very few links*'. Remember the central thrust of this book – a performance appraisal process will deliver little, or do real harm, if it does not connect with other parts of the organisation's performance management efforts. Where there is little or nothing else in place, introducing appraisal will be unwise. Performance needs to be planned, managed, supported and reviewed – through appraisal – and rewarded in some way. Simply establishing a reviewing mechanism through performance appraisal when the other components of performance management are missing or faulty will do little or nothing positive for individuals, their managers or the organisation.

'*To some extent*'. This presents designers with a difficult task. They may be under pressure to proceed because there is some evidence that other components of performance management are in place. They will need to work out just how weak or strong is the link between appraisal and other aspects of the performance management process and make their recommendations to senior managers or whoever is the appraisal process's sponsor.

'*There is good linkage*'. In this case all may be well, but my experience suggests that designers still need to be alert. They may believe they are installing components that will fit into place with little or no difficulty. This may not be the case. My preference is to think of the process as organic and cultural, a much less mechanistic and probably a more helpful metaphor.

If other mechanisms exist, such as planning, managing and support and reward, then there is every possibility that informal appraisal processes are also in place. Therefore, rather than installing a new component we are in the business of cleaning, renovating and upgrading the existing one.

The closer one gets to implementing an appraisal process the clearer becomes the picture of the degree of linkage with the other aspects of performance management. As the picture becomes clearer, designers should revisit the appraisal process's purpose in relation to the other aspects – coaching, measurement and so on, and ensure that the appraisal process and other components of performance management are realigned.

relationship between appraiser and appraisee

Answers to Key Questions 1–5 will have implications on the relationship between appraiser and appraisee in the appraisal discussion. We have established that it is important to be aware of the existing relationships between appraiser and appraisee. This applies both when performance appraisal is being introduced and when formal performance appraisal processes are already in place.

key question 6

what are the implications of the decisions on intent and purpose of the appraisal process in general and on the relationship of appraiser and appraisee in particular?

The purpose of an appraisal process can place very high demands on appraiser and appraisee and designers must consider these demands. In some organisations, only a few appraisers and appraisees may have or can readily develop the skills to run the appraisal process. If that is the case designers need to rethink the purposes and to end up with answers to Key Questions 1–5 that lead to realistic demands and a workable relationship between appraiser and appraisee.

The message is blunt: if the intention behind and purpose for performance appraisal is wrong for an organisation, it will not develop a workable process.

the key questions interact

Figure 5.1 represents a *system* of interactive relationships between the questions. For example, if the process should protect the total confidentiality of an appraisal discussion, a possible issue within Key Question 3, would that impede the generation of training and development plans, a possible issue within Key Question 5?

The answers to the six questions above need to be laid side by side. This helps to surface tensions between the responses. The tensions need to be reduced before deciding the appraisal process's purpose.

Rather than confronting the tensions some organisations ignore or 'fudge' issues. Also they skirt around issues and water down the process' purpose in order to make the process accept-

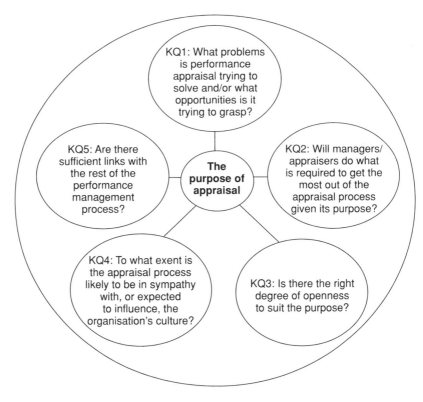

KQ6: What are the implications of all these areas on relationships, particularly between appraiser and appraisee?

KQ = Key Question

Figure 5.1 *Deciding on the purpose of appraisal – Key Questions*

able. This often leads to a process that is of little value to individuals, managers or the organisation as a whole.

deciding nature and scope

The appraisal discussion is the most obvious manifestation of the appraisal process. Those things that are deemed appropriate or inappropriate within the appraisal discussion give a good indication of the nature and scope of the appraisal process.

Having seen a large number of appraisal processes and discussions in action, it seems to me that processes fall into one of three broad approaches. These are shown in Figure 5.2, which presents content and consequences of different types of appraisal discussion. It also suggests that different organisation cultures are likely to react differently to each approach. It does not, however, recommend the three models. There is no one best approach. All three have their strengths and weaknesses.

The approaches are contrasted in this chapter.

Further variations are possible within each approach. For example, under the *assisted self-review* approach, the appraiser could be a peer or anyone inside or outside the organisation that the appraisee finds helpful. It is also possible to base the appraisal discussion on the competencies that are believed to be exhibited by an effective job-holder with, or without, discussing what the appraisee contributes to the organisation.

The *performance improvement* approach can proceed in a variety of ways. For example the setting of objectives for the next period can be part of the appraisal discussion, but can also take place at a separate meeting, shortly after the appraisal discussion proper. Also, the approach can include, but does not require, an overall rating of the appraisee's performance.

The *performance assessment and planning* approach can contain evaluations against competencies and performance objectives, as well as some overall evaluation of performance.

Scope of Appraisal Discussion	Potential appraiser Orientation	Nature of Coverage	Outcome	Attractive to:
Assisted Self-Review	Acts as facililitor and sounding board. Draws on counselling-type skills. Some, little, or no voicing of own opinion. Amount of input guided by appraisee.	Left to the appraisee to define, but typically concentrates on the individual's development needs/goals and career development. May or may not include reflection on performance but related to the organisation's need.	Personal development plan which the individual then needs to find a way of resourcing. May include overall performance rating.	Caring HR cultures.
Performance Improvement	As for assisted self-review some of the time PLUS discussion of evaluations of performance. Information gathered from various sources, eg quantifiable results, documentation, observation and discussion.	Wide-ranging with a shared and agreed agenda within the process's framework, eg the process may require detailed career discussion to be held on a separate occasion.	Measurable performance improvement targets. Agreed, resourced, training and development plan. Realistic but challenging performance rating for the period under review.	Integrated HR cultures would be interested in well-designed and conducted performance improvement processes. Apathetic HR cultures would pretend they are interested.
Performance Assessment and Planning	As for assisted self-review and performance improvement some of the time PLUS overall rating of performance and implications of the rating on pay, promotion and, possibly, reassignment or continued employment.	There is potential for the same ground to be covered as in the other two approaches. However, because of the implications of the performance assessment, the judgmental role of the appraiser can, too often, dominate the appraisal discussion.	Performance rating and recommendation or decision on the person's future. Training and development plans, if any, are short-term. Performance objectives for next period.	Exacting HR culture.

Figure 5.2   *Three approaches to the nature and scope of the appraisal discussion*

Having identified three broad approaches that have an impact on the nature and scope of the appraisal discussion, we can now look in more detail at the decisions that need to be made and the Key Questions that arise, in consciously defining the nature and scope of the appraisal discussion.

key question 7

what will be appraised, and why?

We are back to the 'What's in it for me?' issues. What does the appraisal need to cover to satisfy the interests of the organisation, the appraiser and appraisee?

Appraisers and appraisees are most likely to use an appraisal process when it covers themes that they consider important – those things that will make their jobs meaningful, enjoyable, easier – or whatever it is that interests them. Appraisal process designers may not be able to meet all of the participants' needs all of the time. However, the challenge is to get as close as possible and to be clear when and why some of the participants' needs will not be met.

Answering the 'Why?' in Key Question 7, and asking it regularly, pays dividends.

The decision as to what is or is not within the scope of appraisal must reflect the answer to Key Question 1: What problem is performance appraisal trying to solve and/or what opportunities is it trying to grasp?

For example, an organisation in relatively stable conditions may find its needs are met by appraising against a job description and nothing more. This contrasts with an organisation that is competing fiercely in a tough, rapidly changing market. The need to stay ahead of its competitors is likely to mean that it would be better served by using measurable output objectives for each individual's performance which are updated through regular monitoring sessions.

The appraisal processes I have seen succeeding in recent years are those that are flexible. They take account of changes in the organisation's priorities as well as attend to longer-term issues and design. The appraisal process and its surrounding performance management practices that can be adjusted can keep pace with and facilitate change. Once the decision on what is to be appraised has been taken, it is necessary to decide who to involve in various stages of the appraisal process. To help us do this we need an idea of how appraisal is intended to fit into a performance management cycle (as shown in Figure 5.3).

key question 8

who should be involved, and what are their responsibilities?

Here we will consider the response to the question by examining the major components of performance management that immediately surround performance appraisal: performance planning; monitoring and recognising performance; supporting performance; the appraisal discussion; and reward and recognition.

Involvement in planning performance. Does planning need to involve the appraisee other than to inform him or her what is expected? Would organisations dream of leaving the appraisee out of the performance planning process? Is it essential to involve someone above the appraisee in the hierarchy? If the individual has all the necessary information – clarity of direction, a list of agreed competencies, etc – could or should the planning be left to the individual?

Should the job-holder and the person who will eventually conduct the appraisal share the task of formulating a performance plan? Or, in conventional hierarchies, should the line manager's manager become involved? Although most appraisal discussions are conducted by a person's line manager, this does not mean that the planning process has to be the appraiser's responsibility. As we move away from traditional hierarchies, the choice of who gets involved in planning performance needs

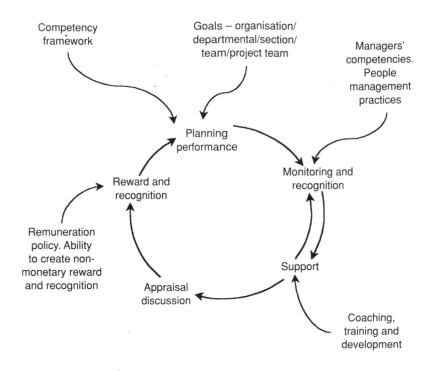

Figure 5.3 *A performance appraisal cycle and links with performance management*

to be thought through. All these questions deserve considered answers and the answers will set the tone for the appraisal process.

People who report to, or feel as though they report to, more than one person need some reassurance that they will be operating against a reasonably robust set of performance criteria. Understandably, they do not want several people arguing months later that the criteria were wrong in the first place.

Whatever the decision, it is important to be clear about who the appraisers are, and what their contribution and responsibilities are within the process.

Involvement in monitoring performance and recognising progress. When the line manager is also the appraiser it seems obvious that he or she should accept the responsibility for steering the appraisee through one, or preferably more than one, monitoring session during the performance management cycle. Potentially, several people could contribute to establishing how well the plan is working out in practice. For example, the line manager, who may also be the appraiser, the appraisee, colleagues, customers and suppliers could all contribute to monitoring and recognising performance.

When the measures built into the planning process are sufficiently robust, then anyone who knows the plan and can access the data can note actual performance against that which was planned. Self-monitoring against quantifiable objectives becomes possible. In some organisations that is sufficient; in others the recognition that the line manager can give to the appraisee is regarded as one of the benefits of monitoring. In this case the line manager will be involved even though the data speaks for itself.

In cases where progress is not as good as was hoped for, it is necessary to decide three things: if this is acceptable; if improvements are necessary; and if so who is to do what?

The line manager/appraiser could take on the responsibility of working with the job-holder to explore the causes and work with the appraisee to define remedial action. Alternatively, appraisees can be asked to come up with their own analysis or solution.

Less quantifiable goals may need different data, for example the systematic gathering of opinions in order to monitor progress on the extent that competencies are exhibited or are being acquired. If handled well, 360° feedback can be very useful and powerful (see Chapter 8). Therefore, although it may seem sensible for the line manager to be a key figure in monitoring, there are additional, if not alternative, players who could be involved. We will consider the frequency of monitoring discussions later in this chapter.

Involvement in supporting performance. The support provided alongside monitoring is a feature of some approaches to performance management. Again, most organisations believe there are clear advantages to be gained from the person's line manager taking on this supportive role, especially when the manager is also the appraiser. However, there are alternatives.

There are two strands to support: defining what is necessary and providing the support. Most performance management processes seem to expect the line manager, when he or she is also the appraiser, to operate in both roles. There are cases, though, where the line manager may be able to help define what support is required, but the provision of that support could involve other people. Having a sales director work out who needs what support and also provide much of the support to sales people is a straightforward arrangement. A non-technical line manager and appraiser of a technical specialist, however, may not be able to identify with the person the sort of support they need, nor provide it: the appraiser may not have the expertise. Decisions need to be taken as to who, if anyone, will help the job-holder to identify this, and who will provide it.

Involvement in performance appraisal. It is critical to involve the appraisee. His or her contribution to the appraisal process is what makes it work.

The nature and success of appraisal depends a great deal on what appraisees believe to be the reason for their involvement. Those beliefs can make or break an appraisal process. Appraisees may believe that there is a genuine interest in involving them in the appraisal process. Alternatively they might, quite understandably in some instances, believe that their input is insignificant, for example, when they think they are brought into the process in order to give them a *sense* of being involved.

In some organisations the line manager's responsibility is to provide his or her boss with information because it is the super-boss who conducts the appraisal. This can be variously interpreted as the appraisal being so important that the super-boss does it, or that the manager can't be trusted, or that it is an attempt by the organisation to overpower the appraisee by having the appraisal conducted by a senior person.

In a minority of organisations a panel handles the appraisal discussion. The panel may include the individual's functional manager and one or more project managers. In other project or matrix organisations the views of others are sought and the appraisal led by the functional manager or a project manager. What needs to be clear is who is responsible for preparing for and conducting the appraisal discussion. Whatever the choice, a message will be sent by the organisation.

Involvement in reward and recognition. A critical part of performance management is the appraisee's knowledge of what aspects of performance are being recognised and rewarded. The appraiser or another informed person needs to explain carefully why reward and recognition has, or has not, been earned. Whether the appraisal process is or is not pay linked, the degree to which reward and recognition will work as reinforcers of behaviour is directly proportional to the extent to which the appraisee knows what is being rewarded.

key question 9

what are the implications for a performance appraisal process of a link, or no link, with pay?

Most organisations will accept that an appraisal process feels different because there is, or there is not, a link between appraisal and pay. For our purposes there are some key points to address on the often unanticipated, negative, consequences of the decision to link pay with appraisal results and the impact the decision has on the nature and scope of appraisal.

If there is a link between performance appraisal and pay:

- The pressure to produce 'felt-fair', rigorous, measurement instruments increases; a pressure that is rarely satisfied and can lead to measuring what is easy to measure rather than what is important to measure.
- There is a tendency to rely on the link with pay to do the managing for some managers, eg they hope that a pay link will motivate people who dislike their jobs to aim at highly ambitious performance objectives.
- There is an increased need to help people understand what good performance looks like for appraisal to work for the organisation – appraisees want to know exactly what to do and deliver.
- If just a few high performers are rewarded handsomely the organisation needs to deal with the possible demotivating affect it has on average performers; not all will see it as an incentive to improve.

If there is no link between performance appraisal and pay:

- Organisations wanting to see high performance are under more pressure to identify appropriate non-financial rewards to differentiate between those putting in high-level performance and those who are not (it is useful to do this even when there is a pay link but more important when there is no link).
- There may be demotivating cynicism, particularly in highly profitable companies, concerning who benefits from the organisation's highly effective performance.
- Top performers may leave the organisation and join organisations which directly reward superior performance.

The appraisal process needs to contribute to dealing with these consequences. As it does so, the nature and scope of the performance appraisal process becomes defined.

key question 10

will performance ratings be *agreed* at the appraisal decision or will the appraisee be informed of the rating before, during or after the appraisal discussion?

As shown in Figure 5.2, appraisal processes may or may not include a performance rating. If performance appraisal involves performance assessment, a performance rating is required. How that rating is formed and when it is conveyed to the appraisee has a significant impact on the conduct of the appraisal discussion. Both appraiser and appraisee either need to know what the policy is in response to Key Question 10, or they need to know that there is no policy. The question is particularly pertinent when appraisal has a direct bearing on pay.

In deciding whether to adopt a policy, and if so which one, those responsible might regard the argument for and against as follows:

■ The rating is to be *agreed* during the appraisal discussion. On the positive side it may be possible for the appraiser and appraisee to agree an authentic rating. On the negative side the appraiser may feel under pressure to appease an appraisee. The parties may indulge in a negotiation and lose the benefits of other aspects of the appraisal discussion.

■ The performance rating is to be decided after the appraisal discussion. The appraisee is able to inform the final rating but may be reluctant to be open about the help he or she may need to overcome a shortfall in performance.

■ The rating is decided before, and announced at, the appraisal discussion. If the appraisee agrees with the rating the other agenda items for the appraisal meeting could still be profitably pursued. However, if the appraisee disagrees it may be difficult for appraiser and/or appraisee to focus on the other agenda items in the appraisal discussion.

key question 11

how can significant responsibility be left with appraisers and appraisees?

Answering this question involves deciding on who is responsible and accountable for the appraisal process as a whole. In larger organisations is it the HR manager, the senior management team, or those with a remit for quality improvement? Who notices when appraisal discussions are not taking place and what do they do if they do notice? When there are forms to be completed, who gets them to the appraiser and appraisee?

The appraiser and appraisee should share the responsibility for appraisal. Three conditions have the effect of removing responsibility from them.

Firstly, when there are no consequences to ignoring the appraisal process or of merely 'going through the motions'. In other words the appraisal process becomes voluntary in practice even if it is deemed to be compulsory by policy. One solution would be to include committed participation in the appraisal process as a performance criterion.

Secondly, when HR departments are insufficiently assertive during the design and introductory phases the following can happen all too easily:

■ The HR department is asked to coordinate the design and introduction of a new or revamped appraisal process.

■ HR invites managers and other employees to get involved in the design and in thinking about introduction.

■ Those who get involved are unable to commit sufficient time.

- ■ HR compensates for the lack of time.
- ■ Proposals go through 'on the nod' without helpful challenge that would make the process fit what managers and others would find helpful and realistic.
- ■ Subsequently managers and other employees do not operate the process fully and complain that it is too demanding and not helping them to do their jobs.

It is essential to avoid this train of events. To do so takes insight and high-level political and influencing skills. To call a halt to design because the HR department is not getting the involvement it needs tests those skills.

Thirdly, appraisers and appraisees feel relieved of responsibility when HR departments are seen to be accountable for the process. It is common for HR departments to lead the design phase and then administer appraisal processes. They are frequently seduced into being 'in charge' or may volunteer to be in charge. They distribute forms, chase stragglers and generally supervise the process. It takes resolve and some sound tactics to avoid becoming the police force. HR departments need to ensure that they build organisation-wide ownership from design stage to implementation.

The HR section in one of my client companies placed the documentation and forms on the company's intranet and the company's President made it known that he expected everyone to access the material they needed, thereby locating responsibility for carrying out the process with managers/appraisers and appraisees.

Designers of appraisal processes need to decide how prescriptive the ground rules will be.

Some years ago a former colleague told the story of the introduction of appraisal into his army battalion during the late 1950s – a radical innovation at that time.

At his first appraisal interview, as it was called, an experienced corporal marched into the captain's office. The captain invited him to sit down. This threw the corporal. He had never *sat* in a captain's office before. The captain spent a few minutes describing the purpose of the meeting. Towards the end of the introduction he mentioned that the appraisee's view on how things had been going over the preceding year was very valuable. He concluded by saying, 'So over to you Corporal Thompson'.

Corporal Thompson looked puzzled and then sat to attention and barked the question, 'Permission to speak, sir?'

How an appraisal process 'feels' owes a lot to the freedom people have to operate it and the extent to which they exercise that freedom. Some processes are more prescriptive than others. There may be forms that need to be completed in a particular order, or there may be little documentation. Some processes confuse both appraiser and appraisee by indicating that they have considerable discretion and then producing detailed guidance notes and forms for them to complete. In other cases managers are actively encouraged to take charge of the appraisal process to support their activity's goals.

key question 12

what discretion will the parties to appraisal have?

The discretion that is given to inexperienced and untrained managers with few people management skills is likely to be less than that given to highly experienced, socially skilled managers.

Appraisees' discretion needs to be signalled as well. They need to know the prescriptions and proscriptions – what is expected and what is off-limits. Is it acceptable to talk about pay in the appraisal discussion even if there is no formal link between appraisal and pay? Does the appraisee have to attend an appraisal discussion? Can the appraisee raise career matters or is the appraisal just about current performance and planning for the next year?

Whether the ground rules are loose or tight, or some point in between, makes an impact upon the nature and scope of the performance appraisal.

key question 13

what is the relationship between appraisal and disciplinary processes?

Many employees will have heard stories of people being sacked during an appraisal discussion. Whether myth or reality these stories get in the way of constructive dialogue between appraisee and appraiser.

The organisation must decide what link, if any, there is between appraisal and the organisation's approach to disciplinary action. Many books on appraisal urge organisations to state that there should be no direct link between appraisal and disciplinary measures related to unacceptable behaviour or inadequate performance.

To accord the conventions of the confessional to the appraisal discussion takes the case to an extreme and is unrealistic. Even if there is no direct link there is usually an indirect link.

The normal aim is to introduce as few surprises as possible into an appraisal discussion. However, it is possible for appraisers to conduct an appraisal discussion knowing that it will cast such serious doubts on an individual's competence, performance and behaviour that these must be dealt with. Also, serious issues may emerge or crystallise during the appraisal discussion.

I am not suggesting that the appraisal discussion should be converted into a disciplinary session there and then, but the issue that emerges will need to be dealt with in another setting.

Organisations need to plan for this eventuality, so appraisers know exactly what to do if and when the appraisal discussion begins to merge into a disciplinary situation. Appraisees also need to know their rights and obligations.

One of my client companies requires appraisers to think ahead. If the appraiser believes the appraisal meeting is likely to lead to serious disciplinary action, the appraisal meeting will not take place. The manager concerned is required to pursue the disciplinary action in place of the appraisal discussion.

Although a defensive act, a good reason for recording the outcome of an appraisal discussion is that in rare instances both appraiser and appraisee have useful material should disciplinary eventually lead to formal proceedings. An organisation may have difficulty in demonstrating poor performance if an appraisal record is non-existent or if it does not highlight concern about the individual's performance. Conversely, employees will have difficulty in demonstrating that there had been no criticism or concerns raised about performance without an adequate appraisal record to support their case.

design, test, introduce

detailed design decisions

By the time those designing the process have got to the point of making detailed design decisions they should be able to state:

- The anticipated outcome of appraisal in the organisation – problems that should be solved and/or opportunities that should be grasped by the process.
- The extent of management commitment.
- How transparent the process should be.
- The impact upon the process of the organisation's work culture and HR culture.
- The extent to which the process is intended to contribute to changing culture.
- The extent to which the appraisal process will be an integral part of an effective performance management process.
- The intended relationship between the appraiser and appraisee.
- What will be appraised and why.

▦ Whom the appraisal should involve.

▦ The responsibilities of the parties for performance planning, monitoring and the appraisal discussion.

▦ Whether performance ratings should be agreed or announced.

▦ Who is in overall charge of the process, especially the appropriate responsibilities of the HR department should there be one.

▦ The extent to which the ground rules for operating the appraisal process will be loose or tight.

Appraisal process designers must have this information in order to undertake the detailed process design effectively.

is 'a scheme' needed?

'We just tell everyone that their performance will be reviewed by their line manager. Every line manager will meet with those reporting to them for an hour or two twice a year to see how things are going. At the end of that conversation every employee will know whether they are on-track or not and what needs to be done over the following few months and what improvements they need to make in their performance. They can also set up any training or updating that is needed to work on the priorities. Do we really need a scheme with lots of paperwork and so on?'
Chief Executive of a small company employing 40 people.

The Chief Executive quoted above has a point, especially in a small company.

An appraisal process is much more than the paperwork that tends to go with it. The process is made up of decisions, actions and constructive working relationships. The paperwork can be minimal – again, as simple as possible but as complex as necessary. In any case, as discussed in Chapter 8, if individual managers set up their own processes, they can be virtually paper free.

Let us consider the advantages and disadvantages of having a process that is documented. It is likely to include forms and a set of guidance notes on the purpose of the scheme as well as describing the formal procedures to be followed in operating it. The advantages of a documented scheme are:

■ It spells out what the appraisal process is about, so that those commissioning it know what they and the organisation are committed to doing if appraisal is introduced.

■ Assuming people read the documentation, and that it is well written, everyone knows what to do.

■ There is a greater chance of consistency, extremely important when there is a link between appraisal and pay.

■ It increases transparency.

■ It establishes the status of the process.

■ Usually it calls for a written record of outcome and an action plan which facilitates progress tracking and makes it more purposeful

The disadvantages of a documented scheme are:

■ The spirit of the appraisal process can get lost in the words.

■ Appraisers and appraisees may be less candid because what they say could be formally noted.

■ People may stick to the rules and interpret them too narrowly.

■ Once codified, the appraisal process can be more difficult to change as rigidities set in.

■ Detailed documentation and guidance notes can be bulky documents.

■ Those involved may not read, or may just scan, the

scheme documentation with the result that inconsis-
tencies unexpectedly creep in.
■ It increases the chances of a process becoming a form-
filling exercise rather than a purposeful dialogue.

Appraisal processes that have minimal or no documentation
may appear attractive at first sight, particularly for smaller
organisations which can operate effective appraisal processes
with little written down. Excessive bureaucratisation through
an elaborate scheme waters down the notion that it is the
behaviour of appraiser and appraisee that makes appraisal
processes work.

However, with very few exceptions, the absence of some
formal requirements causes problems – when appraisees
change jobs or reporting arrangements, in large organisations
where training and development plans need input from
appraisal, and when people simply forget who was to do what.
Some of the pitfalls of having a documented scheme can be
minimised. Although I have come across 50-page guidance
notes and 10-page appraisal forms, they are not necessary.

Naturally, it is up to the designers of appraisal processes to
make up their own minds on the extent to which a formal
scheme is necessary. They need to be really confident that
appraisers and appraisees know enough about the intention of
appraisal, and support the intention, before promoting a
process that does not have an agreed scheme to back it up.

leading appraisals

At the detailed design stage it needs to be clear who will drive
the appraisal discussion and with what authority. Organisations reach their own conclusions as to who that should be. For
example, the performance management process in English
schools introduced in the academic year 2000–01 sees the
individual teacher and his or her 'team leader' at the core of the
process. This pair undertakes the planning and monitoring that
leads to the performance review (ie appraisal discussion).

In other settings the appraiser's super-boss initiates the process and monitors progress. He or she discusses who would make the most appropriate appraiser with the appraisee – especially important in organisations with flat, project-based and matrix structures.

It is most common for organisations to specify that a jobholder's line manager will be the appraiser, on behalf of the organisation.

supervising appraisals

We discussed in the last chapter that whoever administers the process is highly likely to be seen as being in charge of the process as a whole. At some point a conscious decision needs to be taken.

There needs to be delineation of responsibility between five aspects of running the process:

■ Who is sponsoring and authorising the process?
■ Who ensures that the process is carried out – HR? Individual managers?
■ Who updates the guidance notes and forms?
■ Who handles the administration – distributing forms, photocopying, etc?
■ Who is responsible for quality control – monitoring, updating?

As mentioned earlier, the trap for some HR departments is that their involvement in administering the process may result in them being seen to be the body requiring its implementation.

ground rules and protocols

The devil is indeed in the detail. Two of the important items of detail to be considered are: the frequency and scope of monitoring meetings, and the number of times in the year a formal appraisal discussion should take place.

Organisations that use monitoring and support meetings usually use them to supplement one or two appraisal discussions a year. For example, most UK social work departments use a process referred to as 'supervision'. Supervision takes place regularly; once a month is common, although some social work departments expect managers to supervise staff more or less frequently according to their experience and expertise or complexity of caseload.

Typically, supervision covers:

- A review of how important tasks and/or objectives are progressing and being tackled.
- The individual's training and development, adjusting current objectives and establishing short-term priorities.
- Team development issues.

Supervision sessions are conducted with individuals and sometimes with the social work team reporting to a team leader. This level of monitoring and support can often feel like a series of mini-appraisals, some taking an hour or so to run. They become a substantial part of the organisation's performance management activity as their frequency increases.

The appraisal process will need to indicate how frequently monitoring should take place. The frequency of monitoring will vary from organisation to organisation and from person to person. My experience is that when monitoring is a required part of an appraisal process, a minimum number of monitoring meetings is recommended. This provides some flexibility for appraisers and appraisees who value more frequent sessions.

Monitoring sessions make frequent, long, full-blown, appraisal meetings less necessary and can shape appraisal discussions into an opportunity to take stock and look forward as well as look back. When appraisal ratings determine pay, appraisers can expect to be asked for frequent monitoring sessions so that the appraisee can receive feedback on how close they are to meeting requirements, or how far off-track they are.

When monitoring and support meetings are not common practice, the introduction of an appraisal process may require them to be introduced as well. As discussed earlier, the one-off annual appraisal has limited value because of its infrequency and lack of connection with other parts of the performance management process. It is thus very demanding on the skills of both appraiser and appraisee.

measurement

In his book *Managing Performance Appraisal Systems*, Gordon Anderson describes six common, defensible, measurement methods that are frequently used:

- ■ free written report;
- ■ controlled written report using standard headings;
- ■ critical incident technique, eg where highs and lows of performance are described;
- ■ results-oriented methods, eg where performance against SMART objectives is recorded;
- ■ self-appraisal;
- ■ behaviourally anchored scales, eg to establish the appraisee's level of performance on competencies.

Anderson wisely argues against using some previously popular methods that collect the subjective views of appraisers. Usually based on a 'one size fits all' tick-box approach, these methods are quick and easy to use. They are usually intensely disliked by appraisees who are reminded of humiliating, partial, school report cards. Unfortunately, appraisers can use these methods to get through assessment without much thought. Also, the methods often address topics where the appraiser's knowledge is highly subjective, eg individual personality characteristics. Sadly, many of these questionable methods remain in use at shop-floor level in manufacturing.

paperwork

It is unusual for appraisal documentation to stay entirely confidential to the appraiser and appraisee. Depending on the nature and the scope of the process, an appraisal can produce an assessment of performance and/or competencies used for pay purposes, a statement of the training and development needs of the individual and a statement of priorities for the next period. All three of these outputs could go to different people.

Whatever the decision, a decision needs to be made. If it is not made, some people will produce multiple copies of all the documentation, others will copy some pages and send them to appropriate people and others will share no information whatsoever. Inconsistency of practice does little to placate those who are anxious about the extent to which confidentiality is being respected.

disagreement over records

Who confirms that the document is an accurate reflection of the outcomes of the appraisal discussion? What happens if the appraisee disagrees with the appraiser's assessment of performance?

Most appraisal processes I have known in recent years call upon the appraiser and appraisee to agree the appraisal record, especially the main conclusions and outputs. Allowing the appraiser to be the unchallenged author of the record destructively underlines the essentially unequal relationship between appraiser and appraisee. It reduces the chances of the appraisal being felt to be fair.

To be practical, either the appraisee or the appraiser needs to draft the documentation. Which one? Does it matter? Is there a need for consistency? It helps if designers propose answers to these questions, even if practice varies, by agreement, in reality.

Occasionally the appraiser and appraisee cannot agree and one, other or both will not sign-off the documentation. What then? The larger the organisation the more pressure there is to have a policy sorted out in advance. Smaller organisations may delay establishing a protocol until a stalemate arises.

There are obvious solutions. The super-boss can hear the point of view of both parties and reach a conclusion. Grievance, or complaints, procedures can be invoked and in some instances representatives and/or unions can get involved. As the issue escalates, however, the benefits of the appraisal process to the appraiser and appraisee begin to decline.

the official agenda

Both appraiser and appraisee need to know what they are and are not expected to cover during the appraisal, or need to know that the choice of what is covered is up to them. The extent to which they can choose is strongly influenced by the anticipated outcome of the appraisal discussion, eg is the discussion intended to lead to:

- a performance rating against objectives and tasks in the performance plan;
- a competency assessment;
- a training and development plan;
- setting objectives and priorities for the forthcoming year?

tensions

There may be tensions between the timing of appraisal discussions, the number of appraisal discussions an appraiser can be expected to conduct, and how long an appraisal discussion should take. How will these tensions be resolved?

Appraisal usually generates an output that is used by other people in the organisation apart from the appraiser and appraisee. This usually needs to fit into other planning cycles, and results in pressure to declare an appraisal 'season', a period of time during which appraisal discussions have to take place.

An appraisal season dictates a window in which appraisal discussion takes place. If a manager has three appraisal discussions to conduct in, say, two weeks this may present a realistic workload that can be managed along with the appraiser's other tasks. If the appraiser operates in a flat organisation, however, he or she may have 20 appraisals to conduct. This is an impossible task in two to three weeks unless the appraisal's agenda is very short, the appraisal meeting fairly short and the appraiser relatively free of other tasks.

The timing of appraisal discussions, the preparation time it takes, the time it takes to conduct the discussion and the number of appraisals an appraiser is required to conduct need to be addressed individually and together. These issues should not be glossed over. The decisions taken must not jeopardise the effectiveness of the appraisal process.

Resolving the tension between the variables can push organisations to look afresh at the appraisal process and may result in some radically different methods, eg incorporating peer appraisal, team-based appraisal or a greater emphasis on self-review. However, pragmatic solutions to resolving the tensions can lose sight of the purpose of the appraisal discussion. The object is to have a fruitful conversation that maintains or improves performance and engagement with the organisation. The object is not just to get the appraisal discussion over and done with as an end in itself.

pre-meetings

My work on appraisal suggests that there is a trend, at least in the UK, for the appraiser and appraisee to have a short meeting a week or so before the appraisal discussion proper. At the pre-meeting they agree the areas the appraisal discussion will cover, agree what information needs to be exchanged before the discussion or brought into the appraisal meeting, and agree who needs to be consulted for an opinion on the appraisee's performance. There is increasing interest in the use of system-atic gathering of opinion on performance through 360° feed-back (see Chapter 8), and this needs to be arranged.

Preparing for an appraisal discussion through a pre-meeting goes a long way to reduce the likelihood of the parties being disturbed by surprises in the appraisal discussion proper. The argument against is that the pre-meeting takes up time that is more profitably used in the appraisal discussion itself. If the appraiser and appraisee have an ongoing dialogue about work and performance then each will have a good idea of what the other is likely to raise, making a pre-meeting unnecessary.

what does the appraisal process look like?

At some stage it is very helpful to write down and graphically represent the appraisal process so that everyone can see and understand it. An example, but not a model, of how appraisal process can be represented appears in Appendix 1. It will not find all of the flaws: we will see in Chapter 8 that the process still had some undetected flaws when it was implemented.

A flowchart or some other means of following the steps in the process helps those involved to see the extent to which appraisal fits into the overall performance management process, and to spot the connections and disconnections. Remember the lungfish! Some final adjustments can be made to prepare the process for testing and introduction.

Knowing what the process looks like at the start helps to accommodate or evaluate any proposed changes to it during testing and the early stages of introduction or revision.

documentation and/or electronic 'paperwork'

This topic has very deliberately been left to the end of this chapter. All too often this is where some appraisal designers start! That is how designers create 10-page appraisal forms. The materials that might support an appraisal scheme include:

- a description of the appraisal policy, eg its purpose, anticipated output, a flowchart;
- a form and/or guideline on how to prepare for the appraisal;
- guidance notes for appraisers and appraisees on how to conduct the appraisal;
- appraisal record forms (see Appendix 2 for an example).

It is essential that the decisions listed at the start of this chapter have been made before developing appropriate materials to support an appraisal process.

Effective appraisal depends upon a constructive working relationship between individual and manager, appraiser and appraisee. The procedures and paperwork should support, not hinder that relationship. Appraisal designers must work with this principle in mind.

test, train, introduce or relaunch

testing the draft process

Before 'going live' an appraisal process needs to be tested. There are two important reasons for this. Testing gauges the extent to which people will operate the process, so that it is introduced only when there is sufficient commitment to operating it; through testing designers also check the technical aspects of the process for validity and acceptability, eg the rating scales, forms, the guidance notes.

I am often asked by clients, 'Will the appraisal scheme work?' My reply is another question, 'Will your people work it?'

Modest schemes that are used effectively by the majority of people are superior to innovative, technically superb, appraisal schemes that few people are prepared to operate. Testing helps to find out the extent to which people will be prepared to use the process.

The need for testing is likely to be minimised if the process has been designed by a group well in tune with the views of potential users. It is possible for the design group to believe it has measured the organisation's pulse when in reality it is out of touch. Sometimes 'group-think' takes over and, beguiled by the fact that its members agree with each other, the design group loses sight of the views and needs of the rest of the organisation. A scheme can be designed that is unacceptable to the rest of the organisation. This may not emerge before implementation unless the group has the humility to test out its ideas.

If one person or a small group has designed the process without involving potential appraisers and appraisees, it would be reckless to proceed without arranging for them to evaluate it and to suggest improvements.

An appraisal process can be tested by:

■ the person or persons sponsoring its development – typically members of the top team;
■ the process users – typically appraisees and appraisers;
■ those other than appraisees and appraisers who will use the process' output, eg the person responsible for coordinating training and development, strategic planners;
■ those who will use performance data to determine pay increases;

▓ those in a position to judge whether the proposed process makes appropriate links with the rest of the performance management process.

The following methods can test out an appraisal process:

▓ Making a formal presentation of the main features and implications, sufficient for people to be able to demonstrate that they will support the process and sufficient for them to express informed reservations.

▓ Asking people to read and comment on the draft guidelines, forms and any other documentation.

▓ Commissioning some people to undertake a pilot, to try out the process in simulation or for real.

▓ Being alert to people's views in training as the process is being introduced.

▓ Drawing in external performance management/ appraisal experts who can gather unattributable opinion.

Usually, the best approach is to identify and involve opinion leaders, including those who oppose appraisal or have substantial reservations about the proposed process.

The organisation new to appraisal will probably find it easy to persuade people to test the processes. It may be harder, though an equally valid aim, when the process is being relaunched or amended.

launch

A launch or relaunch needs a 'champion': someone who has an informed belief that appraisal can contribute to the organisation and who is respected or has enough authority to command attention.

It is easy to underestimate the difficulties of relaunching or modifying an appraisal process. Though there may be consensus that the appraisal process needs to change, there are no guarantees that the changes will remedy the problems with the current process.

The word 'launch' might imply a discrete, dramatic event that is given high profile. High drama is necessary only when the development of appraisal has been rather low profile, involving only a few of the workforce. Such a scenario is quite possible in large organisations, where it may be difficult to capture the interest of managers and other employees and to keep them in touch with progress on design and development of the appraisal process. In these circumstances the introduction of appraisal does need to be managed, possibly including an 'event,' or, more likely, a series of events.

Little additional activity is needed when the process has involved potential users, there have been open communications on progress, and when designers have been seen to be listening to users' views. This is easier to achieve in open, smaller organisations, where appraisal can be successfully introduced with minimum fuss.

My experience is that it is fairly easy to introduce appraisal in organisations that already have several components of a performance management process in place. In these cases appraisal is perceived as a natural extension of performance management. It is presented as building on good practice that blends into the organisation's existing practices, rather than as a major initiative that needs to be levered into place.

training

Providing those involved with high-quality training for the introduction or relaunch of a scheme is a sound investment, both as a test-bed, and as a way to address the development needs of those involved.

Training can act as a test for fine-tuning the process as well as equipping participants to use it. As people get closer to the reality of appraisal they become more attuned to how the process might work in practice. During training they often begin to notice gaps in appraisal policy that may not have surfaced during earlier information or consultation sessions. There may be some last-minute challenges as well. Therefore, there needs to be a method for recording and responding to the last-minute policy matters and challenges.

Training may also be essential for helping to equip participants with the skills needed to approach the appraisal process, and particularly appraisal discussions, with confidence and competence.

Some appraisal discussions will feature as among the most demanding encounters experienced by appraisees and appraisers. The effective appraiser uses a depth and versatility of skills to clarify the purpose of each appraisal discussion, to structure it and conduct the face-to-face conversation. Some managers simply do not posses these interpersonal skills. The challenge for trainers is to identify the training needed to meet the learning needs of individuals. The 'sheep-dip' approach, where one standard training course or even less, a short briefing, is provided for all is unlikely to equip everyone. Special support, such as one-to-one tutorial support or additional training may be required by some.

Similarly, some appraisees need tailor-made help to build their confidence to engage constructively in the appraisal process and discussion, and get maximum benefit from it.

training for whom?

Some form of training needs analysis has to be done to establish 'who needs to learn what'. Appraisers, appraisees and others who act on information coming out of appraisal need to know how to operate.

I have seen enormous benefits of conducting joint training for appraisees and appraisers. It demystifies the appraisal process and demonstrates that it will work best if both parties will play their part in making it work. Training appraisers separately with different learning goals, on the other hand, usually introduces or increases suspicion.

training in what?

Training needs to deal with the:

■ scheme;
■ structure;
■ skills and styles;
■ sentiments.

Scheme. Everyone involved in appraisal, including those who will use the data coming out of the process, needs to know and understand the system and their part in it. They need to know what preparation will be required and how to use any documentation that is part of the scheme. They will need to know who is expected to lead the appraisal, the topics to be covered and the output required.

Some organisations will make the mistake of merely briefing people on the scheme. They assume that that is all it requires. Some hands-on experience is useful, however. The aim is to get people to use the scheme, not just to have an intellectual grasp of what is entailed in operating it.

Structure. Every fruitful appraisal discussion needs a structured agenda to support the appraisal discussion's goals.

Appraisers develop ways of operating that suit them. Some effective appraisers I've worked with have developed ground-rules for themselves eg:

■ first find out the appraisee's agenda and in particular any concerns;
■ spend no more than 30 per cent of the time looking back;
■ encourage the appraisee to contribute for at least 60 per cent of the time.

Many appraisers I have supported through training have welcomed some ready-made structures they can later adapt for their own purposes. Most ask for a structure to manage the start of the discussion and for the overall appraisal discussion.

Most appraisers will need to find ways of reminding appraisees of the purpose of an appraisal discussion. The mnemonic that appears below is one way of managing the early part of the appraisal discussion.

Starting the appraisal discussion

Talk about

Format – the shape and sequence you will follow

Objectives – the point of the discussion

Note taking – explaining why you as appraiser will take notes

Duration – agreeing the length of time the discussion should take

---

A further mnemonic suggests a way of structuring the appraisal discussion. It has helped appraisers and appraisees I have trained.

Structuring the appraisal discussion

The discussion should cover

Reflections on performance, eg against targets, objectives, competencies, accountabilities, training and development goals

Improvement plans

Targets, competencies, accountabilities, training and development goals for the next period

Actions by appraisee and/or appraisers – who will do what, by when

---

Skills and styles. Appraisal and appraisal discussions need to be planned. Most people need to practice how they will prepare. They might benefit, for example, from undertaking a dummy run at using a preparation form, or being supported in identifying the data they will need in order to make an appraisal rating.

Individuals and their managers may not be used to defining and writing performance objectives that conform to SMART criteria. Both parties may need some training in how to do this.

Appraisers usually influence the 'feel' of an appraisal discussion. The style an appraiser adopts usually depends upon their beliefs on the purpose of the appraisal and the appraisal discussion and their habitual management style.

An indication of the skills most appraisers can be trained to develop in using a particular style can be found in Norman Meir's book *The Appraisal Interview: Three basic approaches*. In his seminal research Meir identified three approaches commonly adopted by appraisers, each underpinned by different sets of interpersonal skills. We will refer to these as the Tell and Sell, Tell and Listen and Shared approaches and consider their implications for the appraiser in the first instance.

The Tell and Sell approach is used to communicate and persuade the appraisee to accept an evaluation of his or her performance and goals for the future. For this approach to work the appraiser needs to have the skills to present and persuade. The appraiser also needs the skills to judge whether an appraisee would be prepared to accept such a direct approach.

In the Tell and Listen approach the aim is to communicate tentative performance evaluations, which can be modified as a result of the appraisal discussion with the appraisee. Appraisers adopting this approach need to be good at presenting, listening, and dealing with their own and the appraisee's emotions.

The Shared approach aims to provide an opportunity for the appraiser and appraisee to focus on stimulating the growth and development of the appraisee, and to some extent the growth and development of the appraiser. The task is to share in solving problems and the grasping of opportunities. To do this well requires a high level and extensive repertoire of interpersonal skills from the appraiser. The Shared approach is not a soft option. It can require the appraiser to be confrontational and challenging as well as understanding and supportive.

To be able to operate some appraisal processes the three approaches need to be combined. It takes great skill to operate in this way. For example, it takes some doing to announce a contentious non-negotiable performance rating (Tell andListen and/or Tell and Sell) and then switch in to searching for ways to support the appraisee to grasp some new opportunities (Shared).

Those responsible for providing training for appraisal skills also need to recognise that appraisees may also need to adopt similar strategies and combinations of the three strategies. They too can present their own view of their performance and seek to justify it, present a tentative self-rating and listen to the appraiser's reaction, or invite the appraiser to share in working on performance problems and opportunities.

Sentiments.   There are emotions, often powerful emotions, at play during appraisal discussions. Most appraisees will react against performance assessments that they believe to be inaccurate and unfair. Excessively unfounded positive ratings can defeat the purpose of appraisal discussions just as much as ill-informed, negative rating. The appraisee is likely to feel particularly strongly about a performance rating that he or she believes is unfair and which will adversely affect pay decisions.

Some appraisers are likely to stay on good terms with appraisees. They may be very supportive and positive but resist making accurate but critical observations of someone's progress, behaviour and performance. At the other end of the scale, some appraisers may have a deep-rooted need to control others and exercise power. They are likely to focus on deficiencies, ignoring an appraisee's strengths and how to further develop them. Appraisers who have a strong achievement drive may have difficulty in relating to appraisees who are less motivated by achievement.

If training in knowledge and skills does not lead to effective performance by appraisers, it will be necessary to pay attention to the sentiments and deeply rooted motives that influence the way appraisers think and feel.

training methods

Helping people *understand* the system or scheme can be done by:

■ using written materials;
■ making a formal presentation;
■ practising completing the paperwork eg using a case dtudy or transcript of an appraisal discussion, preparing objectives;
■ modelling, eg examining a well-completed set of forms and discussing the material;
■ critiquing, eg examining a completed set of documents written to illustrate good and poor practice;
■ using the intranet or, for large organisations, a specially commissioned CD tutorial.

These methods are relatively simple and cheap to use. The danger in their use, as mentioned earlier, is that it is tempting to assume that their use alone, ie simply informing people of what's expected, constitutes training in how to implement the process.

Modelling is probably the most influential way of helping people to develop the skills to run effective appraisal discussions. Appraisers who undergo effective and exemplary appraisal discussions with their appraiser are far more likely to do a good job of it themselves than if their appraisal discussion was uncomfortable, badly run and unproductive.

Naturally, appraisers need to have reasonable interpersonal

skills in the first place. Being party to a model appraisal discussion will not radically alter an individual's interpersonal skills. It might, however, indicate the skills that need to be acquired.

Off-job training strategies for developing appraisal skills include:

▓ exercises, eg to develop skills of objective setting;
▓ role play and other simulations with observer feedback or CCTV recording of practice appraisal discussions;
▓ off-the-shelf video material;
▓ specially commissioned video material.

Appraisers and appraisees tend to respond better to material and exercises that are similar to their day-to-day experience. This material will not always be available off-the-shelf but it is possible to have such material tailor-made. Organisations with large numbers of people to train are more likely to be in a position to do this than smaller organisations. My experience of producing tailor-made training materials suggests that a 20-minute training video may take three to four months to produce from scripting to finished product. Costs vary depending on the production company engaged to produce it.

monitoring the introduction

When an appraisal process is introduced it is essential to plan how its implementation is to be monitored, evaluated and modified. Progress can be measured most effectively when there is agreement from the start concerning the purpose of appraisal and what it is intended to deliver. Demonstrating that the process is being properly monitored and evaluated mirrors the very core of appraisal and performance management: performance is measured and supported against known expectations.

Who will undertake the monitoring and how it will be done must be planned in advance so that the 'monitors' are empowered to undertake the task and recommend any necessary adjustments in the light of ongoing evaluation. This important topic is handled in more detail in the next chapter.

implementing and learning

When the new or modified appraisal process is finally introduced, the work begins in earnest. Keeping in touch with how the process is being implemented is vitally important. The implementation of an appraisal scheme in a fictionalised company – Envirofirm Limited – is presented below. This company is based on a composite of companies I have known over recent years. See Appendix 1 and Appendix 2 for details of the scheme.

Envirofirm's experience

Envirofirm provides consultancy services and products to a niche within the environment market and employs 140 people. The company appointed a group of four people to monitor the introduction of the Development and Performance Review scheme. The group members represented the different project areas and functions, and people at every organisational level covered by the scheme. Through its coordinator, the group had direct contact with the Chief Executive and other members of the senior management group.

Each member had a 'constituency' of 10 named individuals to whom he or she would talk from time to time during the first year's review cycle. This gave the group coverage of half of the company's staff involved in the scheme. The other 40 staff knew that they were welcome to speak to a member of the monitoring group if they wanted to discuss their experience of implementing the scheme.

We will look at each step of the process as it got under way and then, partly based on the company's experience, consider the learning points that might apply to implementing other schemes.

definitions

The appraisal cycle for Envirofirm's Development and Performance Review scheme started with a performance planning meeting with each person covered by the scheme.

The meeting's main purpose was to produce a performance plan which itemised a few key performance objectives for the coming year and a small number of other, less easily measurable, achievements and tasks. The scheme's guidance notes stated that the extent to which performance objectives were met, and tasks undertaken successfully, would determine the merit component of a pay award at the end of the cycle.

Through conversations with their constituents, members of the monitoring group quickly discovered that performance-planning meetings between the appraiser and appraisee were hitting difficulties. The group identified and tackled two issues.

Firstly, although the company's business objectives for the year ahead had already been announced, their implications had not been debated. Some appraisers were having difficulty in translating the business objectives into meaningful objectives relevant for the people reporting to them.

Secondly, most appraisers and appraisees were struggling to find a form of words to express the individual objectives.

Although all appraisers and appraisees had attended a half-day briefing on the scheme, they had not practised writing objectives.

In response, the group arranged for the Chief Executive to run a workshop with all manager/appraisers to talk through and debate the implications of the business plan on all the business activities embraced by the review scheme. It also arranged for a number of two-hour training sessions where most reviewers and reviewees worked on real-life targets with the help of a consultant. As a result of these two activities the scheme got back on track.

The monitoring group identified two cases of reviewer and reviewee failing to agree the key objectives and tasks. In both instances the reviewer's manager was called in, and through a three-way discussion, objectives and tasks were agreed to everybody's satisfaction.

The performance plan for each individual was written down, mostly in bullet point form and usually covering no more than half a sheet of paper. The two parties kept a copy as a live document.

learning points

As we have seen in earlier chapters, defining what is to be appraised can include:

- ▓ activities in a job description;
- ▓ objectives established in line with those of the organisation, department, section, project or team;
- ▓ competencies the individual needs to demonstrate;
- ▓ other behaviours, eg those enshrined in codes of practice.

A successful planning meeting needs information from the rest of the performance management process. If job descriptions are used for performance-planning purposes, some will probably need to be updated during, or preferably before, the performance-planning meeting. Either or both parties will need to know and be able to discuss the objectives for the organisation/department/section/project or team. Competency frameworks applying to the appraisee should also be available, together with relevant codes of practice. The resultant plan gives the individual and his or her manager a touchstone for ongoing monitoring, recognition and support.

recognition and support

Envirofirm's scheme asked the individual and his or her manager to meet during the year to review and recognise progress against the performance plan. During the first year of the scheme's operation, at least four mini-reviews were to be held, as well as a more formal follow-up discussion six months after the performance plan had been drawn up.

The mini-reviews and follow-up meeting were intended to provide an opportunity for the appraisee to ask for support. They gave the manager an opportunity to offer this through coaching and, where necessary, to make other suitable arrangements, eg on-job, off-job or near-job training. The scheme guidelines suggested that the mini-reviews were a good time to celebrate progress and to check whether the performance plan was realistic.

The monitoring group found that most reviews were taking place and their aims were being met. However, some mini-reviews were being rescheduled several times. Also, some managers appeared to resent the time they took (most seemed to last around 30 to 40 minutes) and some appraisees also appeared to be reluctant to meet.

The group encouraged the Chief Executive to 'go walkabout'. He walked around the building several times during one week, just to talk about how the mini-reviews were going. He also listened carefully to what people had to say about mini-reviews. He spoke enthusiastically about the mini-reviews he had conducted with members of the management team. His intervention resulted in more, and more constructive, mini-reviews taking place.

As the time for the six-month follow-up discussions drew closer, the monitoring group suggested that the Chief Executive give a 'state of the nation' address. The group believed this would reinforce understanding of the company's plans and provide the context that was missing at the time performance plans were prepared. At two sessions he addressed all 140 employees and ran a very successful question and answer period toward the end of the hour-long meeting.

He spoke about progress against the business plan and the modifications that had been introduced to the plan as a result of changes in both the market and in their competitors' activities. He was able to give some insight into plans over the following 18 months. He also took the opportunity to demonstrate how the appraisal process was already having a positive impact on company performance.

The information on the company's future and direction provided a useful context to the follow-up discussions, and the Chief Executive responded positively to a request that he should repeat the exercise every six months. His continued enthusiasm for the appraisal process also increased employees' commitment to it.

Apart from slight delays caused by absence and holidays, the six-month follow-up discussions took place and were reported to the monitoring group as being constructive.

learning points

How the appraiser deals with challenges to the performance plan's viability is crucial. The appraisee may have a valid concern about the plan because it is either too demanding or is insufficiently challenging. Alternatively, he or she may be attempting to make the plan less onerous. Usually, appraisers cannot afford to be seen as harsh and inflexible, nor can they be regarded as a 'soft touch'.

The acid test of an appraisal process that includes monitoring, recognition and support is that appraisees are aware that the performance plan is monitored, and that they feel recognised and supported. Leaving the appraisee to implement the performance plan without keeping in touch with progress can have unfortunate consequences. Appraisees and appraisers may interpret the plan differently and the gap between their perceptions can widen as time passes. However well a plan is expressed it is unlikely to be so well defined that there is no ambiguity. For example, even an apparently straightforward performance objective such as 'reduce rejects by 20 per cent' needs revisiting if the appraisee has no control over the quality of raw materials supplied and that quality suddenly drops.

As time goes by a picture of how the individual is doing against the performance plan emerges. Both parties can identify the extent to which objectives are being met, the steps being taken to improve competencies and the extent to which competencies are improving.

Monitoring can take place through day-to-day observation and as information becomes available. Appraisees usually appreciate some face-to-face discussion because it gives an opportunity for progress to be recognised. Appraisees can be thanked and congratulated, privately or publicly, for work well done, and helped to understand why things have gone well. Monitoring is more than checking that the appraisee is on-track and taking remedial action if he or she is not making progress required in the performance plan. It needs to be inter-active, dynamic, and part of ongoing management, not a bolt-on activity.

Organisations must find ways of checking how this important activity is working in practice and how useful it is to the appraiser, the appraisee and the organisation and its customers.

appraisal discussions

Envirofirm laid down a four-week window during which

appraisal discussions should take place. The scheme's monitoring group was very active during this time. Generally, it found a reassuring picture. Most pre-meetings were reported as being useful preparation for the review discussion. Most staff wanted the reviewer to approach internal and external customers and contacts for a view on their performance. Those who were reluctant to involve others subsequently regretted it when their colleagues spoke about how useful it had been to get feedback 'in the round'.

It soon became apparent that one of the scheme's features was perceived as unhelpful rather than as providing some choice. Instead of insisting that the development and performance review discussion should include agreement of the performance plan for the next review cycle, reviewer and reviewee were allowed to defer the discussion of it until a week or so later. This avoided the difficulty of having to wait for a cascade of objectives to be agreed, from the Chief Executive through each tier of the operation, all within the four-week window. On the other hand, to proceed with the development part of the discussion without the performance plan meant that the discussion on learning goals took place without the context of the reviewee's priorities for the following year.

The monitoring group could not resolve the difficulty within the four-week window. On their advice the Chief Executive e-mailed everyone covered by the scheme suggesting that appraisers and appraisees would need to agree between themselves how to operate, but that the policy would be clarified before the review discussion was conducted in the following year. By this stage there was sufficient goodwill for this interim arrangement to be acceptable.

learning points

Discussions rely on both parties being well prepared and appraisal discussions taking place in appropriate places, where the appraiser and appraisee can work uninterrupted.

Provided there has been interim monitoring, recognition and support and that the appraiser and appraisee have benefited from appraisal training, the appraisal discussion itself should hold few surprises for either party. The discussion should lead to the outcomes for which the appraisal process was designed.

Towards the end of the discussion the parties may agree the performance plan for the next period. Alternatively, depending on the process's ground rules, they may have a further discussion to plan performance for the next period. Allowing this choice does mean that the 'window' for appraisal discussions needs to be realistic.

It is important to acknowledge the problems experienced by the parties in running useful appraisal discussions. Little irritates appraisers and appraisees more than being told that their concerns are unimportant.

financial reward

The monitoring group investigated the practice of reviewers agreeing reviewees' performance rating with the Chief Executive and then informing reviewees of the result. A significant number of reviewees expressed concern about this feature of the company's scheme.

Firstly, some reviewees questioned the necessity of the reviewer's rating being 'approved' by the Chief Executive. If the performance plan was reasonable and the information was available to make a judgement, why this second step of validation? The Chief Executive responded by saying that on this first occasion it seemed like a sensible precaution. Since he had had no cause to challenge any of the performance ratings, he saw no need to continue the practice in the next cycle.

Some reviewees said they had been very guarded about what they said at the discussion. They knew that the performance judgement would be announced after the discussion and assumed that the rating would be decided as a result of the discussion. Some reviewees mentioned that they had been less than open about areas of 'weakness'. They thought that asking for training and development to increase their skills would imply that they were incompetent, and that it would have affected their performance rating. Although they accepted that the rating was meant to be based on performance, they feared that the rating would be influenced by factors other than performance against objectives outlined in the performance plan.

The monitoring group believed that this concern about a hidden agenda was connected to the link between the rating and pay. After discussions with the senior team the scheme was modified in the second year. The senior team made it clear that the link with pay should remain a feature of the company's scheme. A revised recommended structure for the review discussion was agreed. The reviewer would announce and then discuss the rating he or she had allocated to the reviewee towards the beginning of the review discussion. The reviewer and reviewee would then move on to the rest of the review discussion's agenda, with the facility for an adjournment for a few days between the two parts of the discussion if one or both parties thought that would be helpful.

learning points

There is no doubt that the presence or absence of a link with pay affects the dynamics of appraisal discussions. However, organisations cannot have it both ways. They are not guaranteed to have open, relaxed, developmentally based appraisal discussions when there is a pay link; and when there is no pay link they cannot guarantee performance appraisal discussions with a clear signal that performance matters: relatively few appraisers have the high levels of interpersonal skills to handle the paradox with aplomb. As discussed in Chapter 1, the everyday message that performance matters is the best way of making the appraiser's job easier, especially appraisers operating a pay-linked scheme.

The device of separating out pay-linked discussions from the other agenda items of appraisal discussions may go some way towards resolving the tension. However, even if the pay-linked discussion is separated by several months from the more developmental topics, many appraisees draw their own conclusions, rightly or wrongly, as to what is going on!

implementing action plans

Some months after the end of the first year's cycle, the scheme's monitoring group noted that although many of the actions agreed during the appraisal discussion were implemented, there were some exceptions.

Training and development action plans were only partly implemented. The shared responsibility for follow-up did not seem to be working well, except in the case of internal support through, for example, coaching and tutoring. There was no coordinated attempt to meet off-job training needs. Few people had the expertise to identify where off-job training through courses was appropriate or how to identify and assess options.

As a result of this observation the newly appointed HR manager was given responsibility for coordinating training. The Chief Executive made it known that the role was to 'facilitate and coordinate' and 'not to be *in charge* of training'. He wanted the main accountability for training and developing staff to remain with managers.

Envirofirm's business results improved during the review cycle. Although it was difficult to quantify the contribution of the Development and Performance Review scheme to the results, the consensus was that the increase in individual, and team, performance was influenced by the scheme being in place and being actively supported from the top.

learning points
It is essential to evaluate the impact of appraisal on the organisation's performance. Large organisations are able to run experiments: for example, parts of the organisation could use

appraisal while others do not, or different forms of appraisal could be used and the results compared. Smaller organisations usually systematically gather opinion and make their judgement based on the information. None of the methods will feel perfect. Organisations tend to have other things to do than to put their energies into developing foolproof methods for assessing the impact of appraisal schemes.

modifying, embedding

Even as a new or modified appraisal process goes through its first cycle the organisation will be experiencing or introducing change, particularly if the environment changes. New pressures and challenges usually emerge, products and services may need to change, competitors and customers may enter and leave the market, and stakeholder demands may change, too.

The appraisal process needs to stay connected to changes in aspects of performance management processes which themselves mirror the wider tasks of managing and leading organisational performance. Appraisal processes create demands on other components of performance management. In Envirofirm's case, the first appraisal cycle revealed that managers' interest and ability in coaching their people varied enormously. It led to an exhortation from the senior team for managers to become more active coaches. Senior managers became more active coaches and also attended the training programme in coaching skills presented by two managers recognised to be effective coaches.

Changes in remuneration policy and practice can have knock-on effects for appraisal processes that are pay-linked. Those responsible for monitoring, maintaining and improving the appraisal process need to examine carefully the implications of such changes. Conversely, the appraisal process may call for revisions in remuneration policy. Envirofirm reviewed its remuneration policy, published it and discussed it with all employees so that everyone knew how pay was reviewed and the contribution performance made to salary.

Keeping connected with other processes is what keeps an appraisal process alive and relevant. If appraisal processes do not adjust then they *should* quickly fall into disuse.

monitoring and evaluating

Rather like the monitoring undertaken by the appraiser and appraisee, the process itself needs some active, regular review mechanism which can lead to informed interventions to change the process. Monitoring the appraisal process provides information that can be used to evaluate the extent to which:

▓ the process is being implemented as intended;
▓ the process is delivering what was intended;
▓ the process needs adjustment so that expectations of it are fulfilled.

The clearer the intentions and expectations are expressed the better. If the appraisal process has ill-defined objectives the monitoring and evaluation of the process and its components will lack helpful rigour. As outlined in Chapter 5, spelling out what the appraisal process is meant to deliver to the organisation, in advance, is the key to sound monitoring and evaluation.

People can award themselves a PhD in hindsight, of course. They can retrospectively decide the purpose or purposes of the appraisal process. However, an authentic evaluation of the appraisal process will refer to decisions that were taken at the design stage.

relevant continuous improvement

After the process is evaluated, those responsible for deciding whether or not to modify it face the dilemma expressed in the three maxims, 'If it's broke fix it', 'If it ain't broke don't fix it' and 'If it ain't broke still fix it'.

Even during the first cycle, if major difficulties are highlighted in the course of monitoring the introduction of a new or revised process, remedial action needs to be taken. Similarly, if the overall evaluation suggests that the process is not performing as intended then action needs to be taken.

If the process is evaluated as being sound and needing little or no modification then the choice is between leaving well alone and changing nothing or introducing improvements, even though they may be very small ones. My experience is that the decision depends a great deal how much improving the appraisal process is seen as key to organisational success. Organisations do not exist to produce perfect appraisal processes. Experience shows that it is unwise to introduce changes that are perceived as unnecessary and trivial by most of those who use the process.

Monitoring, evaluating and modifying the appraisal process should continue after the first cycle. Again, the object is to keep it as an integral part of the performance management process that, in turn, needs to adjust in order to support the overall leadership and management of organisational performance.

special interests

This chapter deals with three special interests: 360° feedback, appraisal that centres on teams, and do-it-yourself approaches.

360° feedback

There is a growing trend towards gathering the opinion of other people on the performance of individuals. Those consulted may include managers, colleagues, internal and external customers and others. This 'in the round' feedback is referred to as 360° feedback or multi-rater appraisal.

Peter Ward defines 360° feedback as: 'the systematic collection and feedback of performance data on an individual or group, derived from a number of stakeholders...'.

By performance, he means the *behaviour* of individuals and teams. In this sense 360° feedback is concerned with what people do rather than what they achieve. The emphasis on behaviour, or 'how' people do their jobs as well as what they deliver by way of measurable results, is what appears to interest organisations. This form of feedback balances out an over-reliance on hard measures on the one hand and the risks associated with an overemphasis on the opinion of just the appraiser and the appraisee on the other. Systematically obtaining feedback 'in the round' can provide rich information to evaluate and develop performance. Most people who come across the idea of 360° feedback are excited and fascinated by it, so much so that some of its demerits tend to be ignored.

pros and cons

When provided by significant contacts, 360° feedback is a powerful tool for assessment and development. Its ability to help people evaluate and benchmark their performance on competencies and 'soft' dimensions is very attractive. Knowing how one's manager, peers, direct reports, and possibly others outside the organisation view one's performance can provide useful, sometimes dramatic, insight.

Managers, for example, could receive feedback on how stakeholders view their ability to plan, take decisions, focus on customer needs, and innovate. The information could be used to support individual development or assess performance for pay purposes. This type of feedback is a powerful supplement to other aspects of appraisal.

There are some drawbacks. Overreliance on 360° feedback can downgrade the significance of performance against objectives – what the individual delivers. It can lead to excessive reliance on the view expressed in the catch-phrase 'it ain't what you do, it's the way that you do it'. It is just one tool in the toolkit and works best when set alongside other methods of assessing performance and identifying learning needs.

If 360° feedback is to be significant, it must be accepted and used by the individual to whom it is given. Some people reject the information because, for example, they are convinced that stakeholders have misunderstood their intentions, or because the dimensions used were irrelevant. In other cases they are simply so overwhelmed by the data that they do not know how to respond to it. Even those who accept the messages from the feedback may not regard it as developmental. They may believe that it is for others to learn to use their abilities, rather than for them to change aspects of how they do their job.

360° feedback requires resources:

- ▓ to evaluate the suitability of off-the-shelf packages;
- ▓ to design materials suitable for the organisation;
- ▓ to introduce the chosen method;
- ▓ for stakeholders to complete questionnaires;
- ▓ to collate results, although this can be semi-automated in some instances;
- ▓ for the individual to read and digest the feedback;
- ▓ to support the individual to make sense of the results;
- ▓ to form an action plan;
- ▓ to implement the action plan.

conducting 360° feedback

Most 360° feedback relies on the individual and stakeholders completing paper-based or screen-based questionnaires. The questionnaires usually cover a small number of fairly open-ended questions or a larger number, say 20 or more, of closed questions. The ratings are aggregated into a feedback report.

The more the questionnaires are of the 'tick-box' kind the easier and cheaper they are to process, but they are subject to the same difficulties as tick-box appraisal forms as discussed in earlier chapters. The more useful, open-ended questionnaire needs a trusted, talented individual to summarise the results. An example of the more open-ended questionnaire and the 360° method I use appears in Appendix 3.

developing 360° feedback

My experience suggests that the following precautions need to be taken when venturing into 360° feedback for the first time:

- Be clear why 360° feedback is being introduced and be open about its purpose: development, assessing performance for pay purposes, or both. It is easy to be enthused by the tool without knowing what it is for and without thinking through the consequences of one's choice.
- Pilot and test the process, and avoid diving in and using it.
- Use criteria and questions that will be valued by recipients of 360° feedback reports.
- Use criteria and questions that will be valued by key sponsors of the process and avoid criteria that are 'interesting' but of little value in moving the organisation forward.
- Be clear on confidentiality matters and avoid guarantees of confidentiality that are impossible to deliver.
- Provide genuine support to people receiving feedback reports and avoid 'dumping' data upon them.
- Hold honest conversations with poor or marginal performers supported by, but not replaced by, the 360° feedback.
- Provide feedback that people can act upon, support them to take action and do not confront them with characteristics which they can do little or nothing about.

team appraisal

Many of my clients recognise that successful performance of some jobs requires individuals to establish good working relationships with many people. Lateral relationships inside and outside the organisation are at least as important as those within the conventional hierarchy, if not more so.

Organisations with flat structures report a high ratio between supervisor/managers and front-line staff. For example, call centres and Social Services' home-care teams have supervisor:staff ratios as high as 1:30. Here it is usually impractical to conduct conventional one-to-one appraisals which are of value within short time frames. If they do take place they are often devoid of useful dialogue.

Even without the pressure of high staff/supervisor ratios, some organisations and managers are developing their own team or 'team-based appraisal' processes in order to cope with the complexities of team relationships with key individuals and with other teams. Team-based processes are used to connect the organisation's aspirations with the team's task and performance. They provide an invaluable context for one-to-one appraisal discussions in most organisations.

The following two examples of successful team appraisal are particularly useful for illustrative purposes. The first exemplifies *team appraisal*, where the *team's* performance is appraised and *team-based appraisal* where the team discusses the performance and learning needs of team members. The second example illustrates, predominantly, *team-based appraisal*.

Example 1

When I worked on an assignment in an electronics company, my task was two-fold: to advise the company on how it should encourage its middle managers to improve the way in which they worked with, and got the best out of, their people; and also to advise on how the company's appraisal process could be improved.

I asked to meet a middle manager who appeared to deliver better results through his team than other managers did. I was introduced to Geoff, the team leader of a group of electronics engineers, who conducted what he called team and team-based appraisal. He and some of his team members explained how this worked.

Twice a year Geoff met the team. As a team they agreed which of their contacts were best placed to give a view on the team's performance, ie who should be consulted, and the topics on which they would like feedback. The topics varied as the nature of the team's work changed.

Geoff then spoke to the contacts and prepared a short presentation for his team based on what they had said. Team members met to discuss the results and also talked about how effectively the team was managing the relationships between team members. They looked forward over the next 6–12 months, recording the work they would be doing and the new demands it would make on the team. In effect, they then identified the competencies the team would need to develop, agreed who needed to develop what competencies, how they could help each other to build the competencies, and what help they would need from outside the team. Geoff reported, and the engineers confirmed, that the discussions were not always full of sweetness and light and that a full and frank exchange of views occurred!

Individual appraisal then was 'a piece of cake' as Geoff put it. The context for the individual appraisal had been well defined. Geoff was able to have straightforward conversations about the 'pluses and minuses' of an engineer's technical ability. They also spoke about how that engineer contributed to the team and what the individual needed to do better in future. Geoff also encouraged his people to talk about how he as the team leader could operate more effectively.

Geoff based the appraisal of individuals on the company's scheme but, it transpired, tended to structure the appraisal discussion much more flexibly than his peers. Most of his colleagues used the appraisal form as an agenda and worked through the items in order. Geoff agreed the sequence he and the appraisee would follow, placing more emphasis on establishing the dialogue than following the procedure. He found that the dialogue was easy to establish because the purpose of the appraisal session with the individual was much easier to agree once the team's performance and context had been clarified.

It is not surprising that the company later introduced both a team and individual appraisal process based on the method Geoff had developed to run his team so successfully.

Example 2

This more recent example is a method used by a local authority Social Services department. Similar methods are increasingly used in other local authorities.

Team leaders of home-care assistants who provide home-based care services in the community, especially to elderly people, use the method with which I am most familiar. The assistants' work includes helping the individual to start the day, administering medication, and assisting with preparing meals and other domestic tasks.

Teams consist of large number of home-care assistants. Conventional one-to-one appraisal was impractical within the appraisal window used by the local authority, and this approach had not been and was unlikely to be used. As an alternative, the Social Services department adopted a team-based appraisal method.

The teams now meet once a year to conduct a team-based appraisal. The team leader outlines the range of work that was undertaken during the preceding year, aspects of the team's task that will be retained during the forthcoming year, aspects of it that will change, and new tasks. There is also a discussion of the team's performance over the year and what the team will need to do well over the following year.

Most of the rest of the meeting identifies anything new that the team will need to learn to do, and in particular the skills that will need to be increased or developed.

After the meeting individuals undertake a self-review of their own training and development needs. They are asked to use a pro forma that was developed with the home-care assistants themselves. Each home-care assistant also self-evaluates his or her development needs and the competencies to be acquired or improved. The self-evaluation is based on a checklist of 22 items of the competencies and training activities that most home-care assistants need to demonstrate and undertake over time.

If they have any items they would prefer to discuss in private, home-care assistants ask for a one-to-one meeting with the team leader. Team leaders also write to comment on the self-review, meeting one-to-one with staff if they disagree withit.

The evaluation of the process at the end of its first year in operation was very positive. The group setting stimulated discussion. Teams were able to cover a wide range of important issues, generate new ideas for how individuals and the team could operate and generate commitment to those ideas. Also, there was an increased commitment to getting the best out of the training provided for a team based on the training and development needs identified during the appraisal meeting. Home-care assistants who feel nervous about undertaking training feel supported by their colleagues.

Team leaders and staff report that the approach is valid and useful and is now a regular feature of how the service is managed.

commentary

The first example illustrates what good managers can do to use appraisal processes to focus on team performance and development. Geoff's team worked together as a group and as pairs and trios within the group. Their ability to work with the team's internal dynamics and understand, contract with, and deliver services to customers inside and outside the organisation was the foundation of their ability to work as an effective unit. Individual appraisal was limiting, if not unhelpful, to Geoff in running his team. There are many managers in Geoff's position who could benefit from organisationally or individually initiated team appraisal process.

The second example features individual self-appraisal that is facilitated by being held in a team meeting. In the Social Services case, one of the motivations for team-based appraisal was the realisation that conventional one-to-one appraisal was impractical.

The success of such a method depends largely on the goodwill of the appraisees. In some organisations, team-based appraisal will be regarded as managers finding an easy way out and being motivated by a desire to save time by avoiding contact with employees regarding their performance and learning needs. This understandable cynicism will be greatest when those involved in the group appraisal discussion do not operate in teams – people know that they are being brought together for the appraisal discussions just to save time. In the Social Services example the four or five members in the group worked in the same geographical area and they could work in pairs on occasions, eg when two people are required to help to lift and move a bedridden person.

The more apparent it is that team-working skill is a key competency the more readily people accept and seek team or team-based appraisal. Team appraisal is most relevant when team members are used to holding each other accountable and recognise the impact on performance of internal team dynamics and the quality of the relationships teams have with other teams. Where people do not have a sense of being responsible to each other as well as the manager they are more of a work-group than a team. When there is little or no prima facie case for a work-group meeting for appraisal purposes then the session is likely to be less well received and less productive than in the teams illustrated in the two examples.

DIY appraisal

Managers who wish to produce their own performance appraisal process usually do so for one of two reasons. Either they regret that there is no appraisal scheme operating in their organisation, or they are dissatisfied with the scheme that is operating.

Some managers are unable or reluctant to spend the time and energy necessary to influence the organisation to make the changes that they would like to see. Instead, they decide to work around the scheme and introduce changes, often unilaterally, rather as Geoff did in Example 1 above.

We will look at the two scenarios identified – introducing your own, or working round a company scheme – informed by Figure 4.1 and Example 1.

where no scheme exists

In this circumstance the manager could pursue seven steps:

1. Crystallise what the manager expects from his or her reports. The manager will need to identify what good performance looks like and to articulate to the team why that performance is required. To do this, the manager needs to know what are the team/department/project goals and how these link to the organisation's overall mission and direction.

2. Decide whether the performance appraisal process will focus on the team, individuals or both. We have seen that the principles applying to the development of processes for appraising individuals' performance can, with little modification, also be applied to team appraisal.

   My experience suggests that when managers have professional employees working to them, such as engineers, accountants or architects, team-based appraisal is at least a good place to start. A year or so later individual appraisal usually follows on as a natural consequence.

3. Establish connections with other performance management processes already in place. All organisations have at least rudimentary performance management processes. People are paid, some training and development takes place and, I hope, there is some clarity about the organisation's goals. The DIY manager needs to map what the existing components of performance management are and the extent to which they will support or challenge his or her ideas about appraisal.

4. Decide how to establish the performance plan for the team and/or individuals and prepare the plan. The performance plan can be based on one or more of the items discussed earlier, such as job descriptions (it is possible to define a team job description), objectives or competencies. Plans for teams can be established at team meetings. For individuals it is appropriate to hold face-to-face meetings. It is helpful to establish a habit of noting the plan once it is established.

5. Give the process momentum by monitoring, supporting the individual or team, and finding ways to recognise performance. The DIY manager can identify his or her own methods of recognising the achievements and progress of his or her reports. The manager can consider using methods the organisation has available – a special mention in a staff newsletter or staff meeting, a personal letter of appreciation, employee of the month awards, for example. Giving some thought in advance to a repertoire of actions that would be valued by the individuals and/or the team will help the manager to provide timely recognition when the opportunity arises.

6. Establish periodic, more formal, reviews or appraisal discussions. Some form of appraisal discussion, perhaps once or twice a year, helps to bring together the monitoring meetings. Most DIY managers I have met tend to *avoid* calling these appraisal meetings. They usually refer to them as 'reviews' or find unusual names for them like 'stock-takes', 'work chats', 'bilateral discussions'. Whatever they are called they are, in effect, appraisal discussions.

DIY managers will need to establish whether and why they are going to rate performance before, during or after the discussions. They are also advised to use some documentation to record the outcome of the discussion and any resultant action plan. They will have the benefit of deciding the support material they need for themselves.

7. Establish in advance what happens to the output. Action plans need to be actioned! Some DIY managers encounter difficulties because they have not thought about the implications of developing a process. For example, they find themselves wanting to agree to reasonable requests for funds to support training and development but do not have the budget and are unable to access someone else's budget.

Developing one's own appraisal process raises expectations. The manager's direct reports expect some follow-through. If those expectations are not met, or the manager is unable to manage those expectations, a DIY appraisal process can have a short life.

day-to-day reinforcement

As discussed earlier, the good intentions of appraisal processes come to nothing if the manager gives different messages through his or her day-to-day behaviour from those expressed during the appraisal process. The secret is to use the appraisal process as a central plank of one's approach to managing. The manager's behaviour needs to be congruent and consistent. There should be no distinction between day-to-day behaviour and that associated with appraisal.

when a scheme already exists

I come across very good managers who want more than their organisation's current appraisal process gives them. When they ask for advice, I tend to ask them five questions:

1. What is the existing appraisal and performance management process? Encouraging the manager to map the status quo means that if they do want to introduce changes, they will at least know what they are departing from.

2. What are the deficiencies of the existing appraisal process and how does it restrict your ability to deliver what you need to deliver? Even though some processes or aspects of a process may grate, bringing to consciousness why they grate is very important. An honest answer to the question helps a manager to know the extent of his or her discontentment.

3. What risk do you take if you unilaterally ignore the existing process and *replace* it with your own? Appraisal processes usually have their sponsors, often powerful ones. It may be cavalier to abandon using a scheme that is valued by, say, a board member or to a powerful figure in the parent company. This is not to advocate blind subservience but to encourage a decent risk assessment before taking unilateral action.

4. What are the advantages of working with, but also embellishing, the existing process? It may be politic or otherwise advantageous to use existing processes but to make defensible embellishments or changes to suit one's own circumstances. Example 1 is a good one: Geoff used the company's scheme, but adapted the structure of the appraisal discussion to meet his and the team's needs.

5. What are the consequences, negative and positive, of asking for approval to introduce your own amendments to the current process? At times asking for approval is asking for trouble. At times not asking for approval is also asking for trouble.

Again, the manager needs to calculate the risk.

As argued throughout this book, when well done, performance appraisal can pay huge dividends. A manager may need to make sure that he or she is in a position to gather in those dividends, going it alone if necessary.

appendix 1

The Development and Performance Review Process for Enviroform Ltd

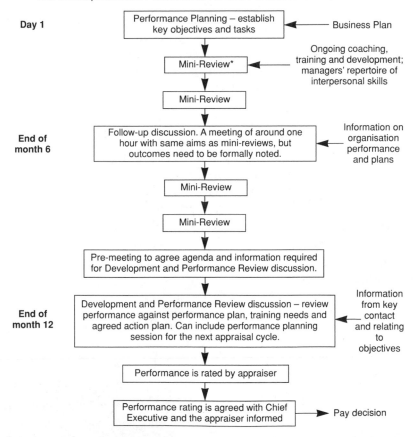

Day 1

Performance Planning – establish key objectives and tasks ◄——— Business Plan

Mini-Review* ◄——— Ongoing coaching, training and development; managers' repertoire of interpersonal skills

Mini-Review

End of month 6

Follow-up discussion. A meeting of around one hour with same aims as mini-reviews, but outcomes need to be formally noted. ◄——— Information on organisation performance and plans

Mini-Review

Mini-Review

Pre-meeting to agree agenda and information required for Development and Performance Review discussion.

End of month 12

Development and Performance Review discussion – review performance against performance plan, training needs and agreed action plan. Can include performance planning session for the next appraisal cycle. ◄——— Information from key contact and relating to objectives

Performance is rated by appraiser

Performance rating is agreed with Chief Executive and the appraiser informed ——► Pay decision

* At least four a year. Can be more. Aim is – to check progress and celebrate achievements, revisit objectives to see if they are still SMART, agree any support required including training/coaching. The mini-reviews should take 30 to 40 minutes, but can be longer if necessary.

appendix 2

DEVELOPMENT AND PERFORMANCE REVIEW
SCHEME – ENVIROFIRM LTD (EL)

PURPOSE AND PRINCIPLES
The Development and Performance Review process is to be
used to support EL's business goals, formally and systematically. It exists to take the company forward.

The Development and Performance Review process will link
business plans with the work, performance and development
plans of individuals. It will also contribute to identifying and
removing blocks to individual performance.

The Development and Performance Review process is
designed to:

- demonstrate to staff that there is a real interest in
  conscientiously identifying their learning needs in a
  systematic way;
- encourage all those with staff reporting to them to
  enter into a dialogue about the individual's performance and contribution to company; and thereby
- assist in the retention of staff.

The output of the Development and Performance Review will
be incorporated into day-to-day management.

The Development and Performance Review will include an assessment for salary award purposes.

There will be *at least* two review discussions a year, one major review supported by documentation and one less formal follow-up where notes of key outcomes are all that is required.

The Development and Performance Review is distinct from the disciplinary process.

THE PROCESS
The sponsor of the process is the Chief Executive. The process should assist managers and staff at all levels to:

- articulate, establish and summarise **performance plans** for individuals over the forthcoming period; the length of the period will vary but where possible it should look forward with a fair degree of certainty over 6–18 months;
- establish within the performance plan, by agreement where possible, an **individual's key objectives and tasks,** thereby identifying what each person needs to do and achieve in order to deliver his or her contribution to the business plan;
- monitor progress through **mini-reviews** and a more formal **follow-up discussion** approximately six months after the agreement of the performance objectives;
- assess the reviewee's performance and what the individual needs to learn to do better or differently and needs to learn to start and/or stop doing through a **major review** towards the end of the year-long appraisal cycle;
- improve the working relationship between reviewer and reviewee; both parties should have a better insight into the reviewee's strengths, work interests and development priorities.

The process will apply to all technical, administrative and managerial staff on EL's payroll. A separate scheme for the production activity is also under way.

Financial support for training and development goals agreed during, and as a result of, the review will be available to staff on payroll.

THE DEVELOPMENT AND PERFORMANCE REVIEW DISCUSSION

The annual cycle will include at least two formal review meetings, one of which is the major review referred to above and the other a less formal follow-up discussion. Both the six-monthly discussions will take place during a review 'season'.

The reviewer will be the person regarded as the individual's line manager. Where necessary, the reviewer will consult other EL managers and staff who have an insight into the reviewee's performance and learning needs. In some circumstances external customers and suppliers will also be asked for their feedback.

The major review, the Development and Performance Review discussion, will have support documentation to (a) help the reviewer and reviewee to prepare for the review discussion and (b) to note the outcome of the Development and Performance Review discussion.

The preparation documents will be completed independently by the reviewer and reviewee. They will then have a short meeting to exchange and discuss the documents and agree an outline agenda for the review discussion. The Development and Performance Review discussion should take place within 10 days of agreeing the agenda.

The major review will usually be used to:

■ Reflect on the individual's performance over the period under review, usually 12 months. This reflection will probably inform the part of the Development and Performance Review concerned with learning/ training/development.

■ Identify and, where possible, plan ways of overcoming blocks to future performance. Blocks to performance can include a wide range of topics, eg ineffective team working, the individual's way of operating, inadequate information, lack of clarity of standards of performance, difficulties with prioritising, collaboration issues with other sections/functions.

■ Tentatively agree the individual's learning/training/development goals. (It may be difficult for the reviewer to commit resources to the goals until the development goals of all his/her team members are known.) Once firm agreements are reached the reviewer and reviewee need to agree who is going to do what in order to implement the resultant development plan.

■ Consider lateral moves or ways of expanding the individual's experience for the mutual benefit of him or her and the company.

■ Provide an opportunity for the reviewee to discuss his or her career aspirations *should he or she want to do so*, ie this is an option and not compulsory. This part of the conversation could note longer-term aspirations inside and outside the company. The reviewee or reviewer may want a separate career discussion involving others in the company.

■ Spell out project or task objectives for the forthcoming period, ie what the individual should achieve over the following 6 and 12–18 months. The statements should conform to SMART criteria, ie be Specific, Measurable, Achievable, Realistic and Time-bounded.

The outline agenda agreed prior to the discussion will shape the discussion. However, because one of the aims is to encourage dialogue, both reviewer and reviewee need to be flexible. New themes and topics may emerge as the discussion takes place and these need to be flexibly handled within the spirit of the review process.

Follow-through actions which rely on the collaboration or agreement of others need to be planned and responsibility allocated to reviewer or reviewee.

The outcomes of the major review discussion will be recorded and be available to the reviewer's line manager and other relevant senior managers. In other respects the outcome notes will be confidential. Copies of the outcome notes will be retained by the reviewer and reviewee to act as a working document eg to monitor progress.

After the major review the reviewer will make a formal performance assessment and inform his or her own manager. The rating will use the following categories:

▦ Excellent performance – profitably attained objectives and profitably exceeded task requirements.
▦ Acceptable performance – objectives attained and tasks requirements met.
▦ Disappointing performance – under-performance on objectives and tasks, need for improvement.
▦ Unacceptable performance – major underperformance, evidence of substantial need to increase competence and/or improve work behaviour.

When the reviewer's manager has approved the rating the reviewee will be informed of the assessment.

For the rating to be felt fair it is critical that the performance plan's objectives and tasks are regularly revisited (a) during mini-reviews and (b) at the follow-up discussion. This practice should ensure that the reviewee should, with application, be able to meet the performance plan's requirements, ie the person should be able to impact upon the required performance.

The follow-up discussion will be used to:

▦ monitor performance against objectives and initiate any required action;
▦ revise the project or tasks/objectives, where necessary;

■ revise or accelerate the implementation of development plans.

The outcome of the follow-up discussion(s) will be recorded in summary form only and held by the reviewer and reviewee, with a copy given to the reviewer's line manager.

At least four additional mini-reviews should take place during the year. The agenda for the mini-reviews is for the reviewer and reviewee to decide. It may include refining objectives and tasks, identifying on-job, near-job and off-job training and development and discussing the demands of and opportunities provided by new projects.

GROUND RULES

The review process has the following conventions.

The company's goals and plans for up to 18 months ahead and further where possible will be clarified with staff before the major review season and reinforced by the reviewer. A performance plan will be established at the start of the appraisal cycle, by agreement where possible. The plan will generate a limited number of measurable performance objectives and a few key tasks where measurement would be difficult or the measures spurious. The assessment of performance against objectives and tasks will be used for pay decisions towards the end of the appraisal cycle.

The review discussions and follow-up(s) should take place as agreed. Only a major crisis should lead to postponement.

The discussions will be held in a suitable room or location; not a pub!

Both reviewers and reviewees have responsibilities. The success of the discussion is not just down to the reviewer.

Agreed actions need to be driven by reviewer and reviewee. The parties cannot assume that the reviewer's line manager will initiate actions unless there is a clear understanding to support this assumption.

There is no intention that the review process will replace

day-to-day task and project management. It should enrich day-to-day contact between reviewer and reviewee. A key purpose is to provide an opportunity to stand back, take stock and plan for the medium and longer term.

WHAT THE DIALOGUE IN THE MAJOR REVIEW DISCUSSION MIGHT BE ABOUT

The following framework summarises the areas to be covered by the review discussion. Typical content of each of the four themes is provided.

Reflect – performance against performance plan (as the process is embedded this will be an examination of the tasks/objectives established at previous review discussions), competence demonstrated, nature of relationships with colleagues and reviewer.

Identify – high and low points ('technical' and other issues), areas for improvement and development, company and individual's priorities over the forthcoming 6–18 months, blocks to performance, career considerations (if the individual wishes to discuss these).

Target – work goals/objectives for the next period, training and development, dates for mini-reviews.

Action – who is going to do what by when, agreed in outline at the discussion and refined later if necessary.

The forms that follow were available on the company's computer network and therefore the space available for making comments could be adjusted by users.

ENVIROFIRM LIMITED

DEVELOPMENT AND PERFORMANCE REVIEW DISCUSSION

PREPARATION PROMPTS – REVIEWEE

Reviewee.................................... Reviewer....................................

Date completed......................................

MAIN TASKS/OBJECTIVES OVER THE LAST 12 MONTHS (will act as focus for review discussion)

MAIN CONTACTS WHO SHOULD BE CONSULTED

MAIN TOPICS/THEMES I'D LIKE TO COVER

BLOCKS TO MY PERFORMANCE I'D LIKE TO DISCUSS

NEW SKILLS/ABILITIES RELEVANT TO JOB/ASPIRATIONS WHICH I MAY NEED TO ACQUIRE

To be discussed with reviewer in order to agree an outline agenda for the Performance Review and Discussion

<u>ENVIROFIRM LIMITED</u>

DEVELOPMENT AND PERFORMANCE REVIEW DISCUSSION

PREPARATION PROMPTS – REVIEWER

Reviewee.................................... Reviewer....................................

Date completed......................................

MAIN TASKS/OBJECTIVES OVER THE LAST 12 MONTHS (will act as focus for review discussion)

MAIN CONTACTS WHO SHOULD BE CONSULTED

MAIN TOPICS/THEMES I'D LIKE TO COVER

BLOCKS TO YOUR PERFORMANCE I'D LIKE TO DISCUSS

NEW SKILLS/ABILITIES RELEVANT TO JOB/ASPIRATIONS WHICH YOU MAY NEED TO ACQUIRE

To be discussed with reviewee in order to agree an outline agenda for the Performance Review and Discussion

ENVIROFIRM LIMITED

DEVELOPMENT AND PERFORMANCE REVIEW DISCUSSION

REVIEW DISCUSSION OUTCOMES

Reviewee...................................... Reviewer....................................

Date of discussion.......................................

Review period............................ to............................

COMMENTS ON REVIEWEE'S PERFORMANCE, *especially on key tasks and objectives.*

COMMENTS ON BLOCKS TO PERFORMANCE *– what, if anything, could be done by one or both parties to remove blocks. Include other items where one or both parties would need to influence other people in order to remove blocks and note what reviewer and/or reviewee will do in order to influence.*

TASKS AND OBJECTIVES IDENTIFIED FOR FORTHCOMING MEDIUM-TERM PERIOD *if agreed at D & P R discussion; if not, complete after performance planning meeting at start of next cycle.*

REVIEWEE'S DEVELOPMENT GOALS *for the next period, up to 18 months e.g. via on or off-job training.*

REVIEWEE'S CAREER ASPIRATIONS, if discussed, and note of any additional advice/guidance the reviewee would value. This section can include longer-term aspirations inside or outside the company as well as noting any aspirations for promotion within the company.

LATERAL MOVES OR EXPERIENCE ENHANCEMENT the reviewee would value and what needs to be done by reviewee and/or reviewer to test feasibility.

Other comments

Signed as a fair record of the review discussion:

Reviewee..................... Reviewer .... Date ....

Date for follow-up discussion in 6 months ....

Date for first mini-review of next appraisal cycle ....

appendix 3

A simple centrally administered 360° feedback process

Each person providing feedback is asked to answer the following five questions, using up to one page of paper to do so.

In your opinion, what does .... (name of person):

- do well and should continue doing?
- need to do better or differently?
- need to stop doing?
- need to start doing?
- need to learn?

A trusted person in the HR/Personnel Department or an outsider collates the material provided by four to six people and writes a non-attributed report. With experience the report usually takes some 45 minutes to write.

Usually, the subject of the report talks the results through with the appraiser and/or the author. The subject prepares an action plan based on the report's key messages.

further reading and contacts

Anderson, G C (1993) *Managing Performance Appraisal Systems*, Blackwell Publishers, Oxford

British Deming Association *Performance Appraisal and All That!*, PMI Ltd, Coventry

Department of Trade and Industry and the Confederation of British Industry (1994, 1997) *Competitiveness: How the best UK companies are winning*, Crown Copyright

Dutfield, M and Eling, C (1990) *The Communicating Manager*, Element Books, London

Handy, C (1978) *Gods of Management*, Souvenir Press, London

Hartle, F (1995) *Transforming the Performance Management Process*, Kogan Page, London

Hudson, H (1999) *The Perfect Appraisal*, Random House Business, London

Goleman, D (1996) *Emotional Intelligence: Why it can matter more than IQ*, Bloomsbury, London

Goleman, D (1998) *Working with Emotional Intelligence*, Bloomsbury, London

Lupton, T and Gowler, D (1969) *Selecting a Wage Payment System*, Kogan Page/Engineering Employers Federation, London

Kotter, J P (1990) *A Force for Change: How leadership differs from management*, p 6, The Free Press, a Division of Simon and Schuster, Inc., New York

Meir, N (1958) *The Appraisal Interview: Three basic approaches*, John Wiley & Sons, Chichester

Newton, T and Findlay, P (1996) 'Playing God? The Performance of Appraisal', *Human Resource Management Journal* 6 (3)

Sethia, N K and Von Glinow, M A (1985) 'Arriving at four cultures by managing the reward system', in *Gaining Control of the Corporate Culture*, R H Kilmann *et al*, Jossey-Bass, a divison of John Wiley & Sons Inc., New York

Ward, P (1997) *360-Degree Feedback*, Institute of Personnel and Development, London

Bob Havard can be contacted on +44 (0)117 977 0050

Investors in People UK can be contacted on +44 (0)20 7467 1900 or www.iipuk.co.uk

The Hambleden Group Ltd can be found at PO Box 16980, London NW8 9WP, England +44 (0)20 7289 4433

The *Profit from Innovation* programme is a tailored, structured programme, designed to involve the workforce in increasing profitability by using simple but powerful techniques to foster innovation and continuous improvement to respond to changing customer needs. More information can be obtained from Bob Havard.